melanated thouGhts

by

AlphonsoWaldron

This is a work of literary thouGhts. The creation of these words are non-fiction. CopyriGht © Alphonso Waldron; 2022 All riGhts reserved. No part of this book may be reproduced in any form on or by an electronic or any mechanical means, includinG information storaGe and retrieval systems, without permission in writinG from the publisher.

(malicious intent will Get you hell sent wrapped with a bow for your involvement in thinGs that shouldn't involve men)

Certain behaviors as men we have to Grow up from like breakinG younG Girls hearts that with no intentions of lovinG them tellinG them lies just to Get a piece of them now that's some of the weakest men the mentally shallow far from deepest men you see men don't chase pussy they chase success boys chase pussy in hopes of fuckinG all of them real men value themselves too much to ever play themselves and put their physical frame throuGh all types of hell just for some old pussy that probably smells real men want women that's doinG for themselves so they can add to what they already built cause boys look for pussy while men want to know their skills cause unless pussy is beinG sold it won't pay them bills so any Grown men who are still runninG after women for their pussies is ill and needs to be mentally and psycholoGically evaluated for real cause to still be doinG the same thinG you did in your twenties in your thirties and forties shows lack of maturity cause men of hiGh standards don't want to stick they're dicks in every woman they see only a man who is searchinG for h.i.v

(we are a nation that has been separated manipulated castrated and turned into an abomination to follow Generation after Generation)

While they play with our lives we sit around playinG playstation poppinG bottles and takinG vacations leavinG our kids vacant to be discriminated and hated by these made vaGrants who either wants them dead or to enslave them we no lonGer have brave men just stuck in their ways men don't have no clue on how to act nor behave men, men who care more about material thinGs than their own children and women who aGree with these men because financial they need them but one that does not take heed of what came before them will repeat the same madness that's before them which is killinG and whorinG cause beinG Good is borinG until they're prison tourinG or permanently Grave snorinG for iGnorinG the God within them for the devils Garments for their evilness they will not be pardon from their lives they'll be dearly departed for beinG cold hearted and mentally retarded and for followinG trends that should have never started but since they forGot they soon be reminded who God is

(after all our traGedies we still treat each other traGically)

When we see each other it's almost immediately and automatically a homicidal casualty but when the white man comes around it's yes sir your majesty now that's what i call blasphemy GanGster in their own community's but when they see the police they Get quite like the sounds in a library can't handle the time but do the crimes so effortlessly but the sentence Given to them will now allow them to reflect all their foolish foolery that will Get them more years than the combined aGe of you and me for their disrespect towards the almiGhty G.o.d the real biG homie nothinG like these biG phony's who are full of a bunch of boloney cause to continue this Generational madness a man would have to be a complete and utter jabroni that needs to be put in the earth were the worms because they are more hazzardous to themselves and others than Germs be they are filthy dirty unhealthy and unworthy to be put in the cateGory of royalty

(most are only committed to the physical of a person not to the mental reason beinG why most relationships don't last because sex alone is not that influential)

When a union is strictly based on sex miGht as well just call next cause that individual will soon be your ex it will Go from talkinG all day on the phone to two word texts from always happy to always vex because no combility was there of no real content just experimentinG with each other like some project treatinG one another like some objects fornicatinG with no spiritual connection nor commitment and to make it more twisted doinG it without protection a lot of these women and men behavior really needs to be questioned because how they act is a direct reflection of their children level of sexual aGGression now they will no lonGer want use their minds now they choose to use their bodies as a weapon abusinG themselves as if there value is nothinG cause one who truly loves themselves just don't GoinG around fuckinG

(we all we Got so ain't no reason for our blocks to be hot with little kids moms and pops GettinG shot)

Why complain about patrolinG cops when it's the crimes done by us that Gives them jobs but with discipline and unity in place that can all be stopped we can expose the Government and all their plots to make us sick then sit and watch us rot i think not it has to stop no more beinG on the bottom time to be back on top connect the dots take back our spot that was stolen from us by jews polish enGlish Germans chinese redneck americans and polacks who are really our ops not no one with the same hue that we Got but some of us are too far Gone and deserve to sleep under dirt with rocks to become plant food for the crops and they deserve a nooses put around their necks and tied in knots for not understandinG that one hand washes the other they will be killed in flocks by their own iGnorance or the cops then buried in a pine box where there bodies will forever be locked

(the younG and the heartless verses all my killdrens)

You see this killinG thinG didn't start with these younGinGs it started Generations before this one and since then they haven't missed one Generation without a murderous outcome riches they Got none but for them murders they can't be outdone from sun up to sun down never without Guns catchinG bodies to them is a form of extreme fun the stomach aches they leave can't use tums bullets erupts in immune systems and all these killinG are mostly beinG done by younG children who no lonGer have no souls in them just numbness and coldness in them for them it's no purpose for livinG cause none was Given there eyes have seen so much violent visions even thouGh they are free their minds are stuck in poverty prison that's why they rather destroy their own neiGhborhoods with hate before they build love in them but they don't know what love is cause for them love was missinG they act before thinkinG shoot without blinkinG until somebody Gets left stinkinG

(from the oriGinals to duplicates from beinG leaders to always followinG and doinG some stupid shit)

Our ancestors Got raped beat and slauGhtered on some Gruesomeness so much brutalness they couldn't elude from it cause they were beinG Groomed for it by the son of sin "satan" who wants our melanated people to lose not win jealous cause him and his minions lack melinan in their skin and that they were not created by elohim but by lucifer who wanted and still wants to be like him so he came in the form of a woman in order to conquer him from within with sensualness until he climaxes on that kinG size mattress then relaxes makinG him believe that he is really is a she the devil is a Good actress touGh actinG like tinactin to kill God will be his satisfaction but the oriGinal Gods cannot be killed by a copies of their faction only a weak God will for the flesh of the devils physical attraction

(what is a race it is a competition so to call ourselves a race is like sayinG we have opposition while beinG in the last place position it's no different than beinG on a suicide mission)

A race has everythinG to do with runninG with a Goal of winninG it has nothinG to do with Gender or weather your a man or woman it was somethinG created by white men for them to keep us foolish it is the achilles heel for us of their choosinG for them to have the advantaGe to keep on abusinG and for us to have the disadvantaGe to keep on losinG and keep from improvinG cause we to busy partyinG smokinG and boozinG these are distractions and it is all of their doinG to keep us in ruins cause while we killinG chillinG and screwinG they are planninG and plottinG ways to Get rid of us the oriGinal humans we were once first and they were last and when we realize who we are and Gain God's consciousness to it they are afraid that we are Gonna return them to it for their acts of hate upon God's children which was for them absolutely stupid now they have to deal with the punishment God is brewing

(prayers without actions will not brinG you satisfaction)

For prayers to come to fruition you must activate it with relentless conviction besides that level of commitment your prayers will never be answered unless you are doinG somethinG with it like GettinG up and GoinG out and Get it not to sit around all day dreadinG so many people are there own problem and they refuse to admit it the reason they're prayers do not Get answered because they don't allow themselves to let it cause the minute obstacles Get in their way they be like aww man forGet it then end up on their death beds livinG to reGret it cause they were to stubborn to Get the messaGe that they weren't born just to exist but they realize that on their exit cause prayers cannot be answered unless there is movement prayer is only one part of the solution the rest requires movinG which will them brinG improvements

(this life we live is all a test to see who will manifest the God within their flesh)

Everyday we Get a chance to rise is the real privileGe the most valuable riches of all the riches is to Get to open up our eyes and continue livinG for so many that opportunity wasn't GivinG but so many of us take our lives for Granted until they are left in anGuish for not understandinG God's lanGuaGe of valuinG oneself and his planet but for all those that do understand this is not even close to God's plan so many of us has put our lives and the lives of our children in the hands of vicious white pilGrims who are now teachers in the white mans corrupted school system which is only there to Get us prepared for newly built prisons this test from God so many of our melanated people are failinG cause they are allowinG their anGer to prevent them from healinG we went from first place to beinG behind trailinG if a lot of our people don't Get their acts toGether they will be victims of their own self iGnorance for their disrespect of God they will suffer many bad experiences for not takinG the test he Gave to them serious God is no lonGer upset he is now beyond pass furious

(it's unfair and ashame what so many parents do to their kids they don't even improve themselves for their kids they absolutely ruin their kids)

So many parents should be brought up on charges for parking their used cars (dicks) inside of broken garages (pussies) without any houses attached to it without education or wisdom to teach to them fluent they just feed them fast foods and give them phones and tablets to be parents to them most of them don't even know what their children doing out there cutting school and being truants now it's too late cause now the streets done got to them now they went from being dream straight a's children to a total nightmare killers and this is due to lack of love and care from those people who had sex to bring them here and expect them to not embrace their living of melanated men disrespecting themselves and the melanated women disrespecting themselves without care when that's all that they see as adolescent children while negative things is all they hear how do these parents expect them to turn out when they was never truly there

(america is one biG public housinG were druG dealinG killinG robbinG and sellinG pussy is allowed in it is sickeninG what these younG children have to witness because in these adults there is no evolvinG)

There is a problem when the minds of younG kids has to adapt to violence because these Grown adults never decided to run the real Game by them like how to communicate without wildinG america is one biG asylum that is strateGically divided thouGh reliGion color and a person finances where everythinG is taken nothinG is handed century after century still no proGress well polished minds now tainted and tarnished from all of the harshness that they have been cursed with without no warninG like beinG woken up from a deep sleep by the radio clock alarminG but these devils could careless about the shock their they just feed them with a bunch of false hope and broken promises how can they not be heartless demons when they were left in the wilderness to be torn to pieces

(foolish is a woman to blame men for the boys that she keeps on choosinG without lookinG into herself for improvement)

What a way to avoid accountability by not takinG part in their own responsibilities to choose men at a hiGher mental capacity than just pain sufferation and traGedy men with better qualities not boys whom enjoy destroyinG their own community's with pure buffoonery from january to january but these women choose these boys then blame Good men cause they rather pick the druG dealinG scamminG street felons with no future put prison and Grave dwellinG instead of choosinG elite intelliGent unique leGends they pick niGGas that end up in the streets beGGinG to have sex with any woman that they see with their God Given lenses they pick boys then expect men that will honor and protect them when those boys don't even love and respect them they constantly neGlect them but i Guess that's the karma cause they once had a Good man but chose to reject him for a boy who just manipulated them to sex them now bitterness corrupts them now it's fuck men because boys Got them preGnant and left them please make it make sense why are they so mad at men when they didn't choose them

(silly is the man that can't leave the block no difference from a crackhead that can't leave the rock)

*A*ny man that rather be in these streets before the home he Got deserves to Get robbed and shot for beinG in places as a Grown man he should not like in spots that he knows is hot just to be around a bunch of used up women with washed up twats and demons that just sit and plot to find ways to stop their clocks with nines with the dots body's drop after sounds of pop pop pop now no more are they on top call the coroner no need to call the cops no more partyinG the whole party flop now they are permanently layinG in a pine made box about to be buried in a dirt filled lot and most of the time it because of worthless w.a.p any real man will tell you that the streets will only do both of these thinGs which is Get you cemeteried or locked and if you don't believe me just watch there is no expiration for the streets but there is one for the body you Got the streets will not ripen you it will only allow you to rot

(nobody played their kids more than melanated parents did)

Always quick to rare their kids but not properly Guide or take care of their kids when they have somethinG to say they don't even want to hear their kids now they are Grown and anGry now they fear their kids they are quick to be parents after the blood is smeared all over them from the dead bodies of their kids from the thinGs they did due to the people they were made by and the traGedy they were born in that tauGht them absolutely nothinG that will allow them to function on levels above all this bullshit the white man can come up with cause when you separate the head from the body that holds it the body starts to do dumb thinGs like act like niGGas and bitches which are iGnorant men and female doGs and then we wonder why we Get treated like criminals and animals look at the shit we on after all our pain and sufferinG why should anyone love and respect us when we do love and respect ourselves born the children of heaven but turned into the children of hell so many of our melanated parents failed

(once your off the Grid you won't end up GettinG thrown off a bridGe for beinG involved in thinGs that will leave you stiffer than dead bodies in coffins is)

It often is truly unfortunate the price it cost to live from poverty stricken homes to kids beinG Given up for adoption at orphanaGes absent from their lives their birth mothers and fathers is so they are lost and misGuided to what the meaninG of life really is cause they were born into a madness their own parents selfishness brouGht them in they never asked to be here two horny people decided that for them without even havinG a blueprint or map for them just trap after trap after trap for them until they day they meet their end in the dirt or some cold prison not just a little bit so many of them never Get a chance to become women and men because before they can make it their lives are taken from them cause knowledGe was forsaken from them by the one who had sex and made them but forGot to raise them but not condemn them

(when you force boys to be men they use Guns to free them)

Hammers they squeeze them cause it relives them from images that deceive them only violence they believe in demons they pretend to be them until the day God cuts off their breathinG for beinG no Good heathens cause all those who are at odds with God he will Get even no ambulance needed just a bunch of people standinG around who could have prevented this madness from happeninG GrievinG Generation after Generation dyinG for no reason but lack of knowledGe of their true existence if they did they wouldn't be so heartless cold and relentless with the only way to be humbled is death or a twenty five to life sentence for livinG absolutely and completely senseless no Guidance no blueprint just a bunch of attention seekinG parents online actinG foolish but have absolutely no clue what their own children are doinG but they know everythinG GoinG on in everyone's else's lives and on them tel-lie-vision shows they viewinG most of these parents are the reason their children lives are ruined cause refuse to actually teach somethinG to them cause they don't know nothinG themselves so they send them to their enemies to school them

(there's heaven and hell in you and freedom and jail in you,you Got to pick the one that you want to have that valuable and total control of you)

When somethinG is not made for you it becomes like a plauGe to you there will be no savinG you once you allow the devils name to be enGraved in you when you had a choice to let God be the leader of you you decided to make the devil make a slave out of you a walkinG talkinG desiGner billboard out of you materialistic niGGas and whores out of you when you could have took that same money to help your own community improve but chose otherwise then have the nerve to complain how they treatinG our youth but what exactly are we teachinG our youth just to Get fly and be cute when we should be teachinG them literacy in finances and there God Given riGhts to how are they supposed to fix the problem if not Given the tools how are they supposed to know about themselves if they are only tauGht the white mans curriculum in school which critical to their mentals and far from influential to their spiritual followinG the caucasian people principles is not essential to our Growth everythinG we learn from these devil worshippinG demons as melanated people we must let it Go

(they display foolish behavior then when they are faced with the consequences they call upon the savior)

The headless don't feel until when they Get their skin peeled and since they don't want to hear a hurt will come to them from which they cannot ever heal for not payinG attention to simple detail and GettinG fake mixed up with what is obviously real these type of people mistake sharks for whales a head for a tail collared Green for kale paths for trails and poisoned food for a meal these are the people that keeps on allowinG melanated people made up history to repeat itself by displayinG weaker versions of themselves for wealth beneath the value of their flesh they done murdered slept and have completely no respect for their health but a hard head makes a soft ass for those whom don't have knowledGe of self problems will follow them wherever they dwell and show them the difference from heaven and hell

(little Girls use their bodies for attention while Grown women use their brains little Girls don't value their bodies while Grown women respect what's in between their leGs)

You can tell the difference between Grown women and little Girls Grown women are intelliGent and know how to articulate their words while little Girls don't know the difference between nouns and verbs they always sound absurd stay on social media showinG off their Gym and man made curves they are no lonGer women they are man made birds but women on the other hand knows their worth is valued more than any shoes or purse Grown women are Gifts to earth while little Girls in Grown womens bodies are absolutely cursed they think with their pussies first those type of shallow minded women are completely the worst attention is what they thirst they have had more men inside of them than the conGreGations at every church desperate little Girls in Grown melanated women bodies who lacks respect for their selves and you can tell by the way they put their body's throuGh sexual hell

(these ain't trap rappers these are Get you trapped rappers cause when they rap somebody GettinG clapped after)

These dudes ain't rap masters they are rap disasters Guns in videos flashers reality crashers because it is only fiction they are after everytime they put out music these kids are dyinG faster and becominG caspers they are food on platters to be fed to dark matters and it Gets harsher like weed mixed with Grabber like beinG hunGry with no dollars a lot of these rappers are the problem promotinG violence in their music they are willinG to destroy their own community's just for finance but for that karma will hold them beat them scold them and bury them all one by one them and their music will fall for their contributions to the cabal weather white melanated short or tall or weather their so called reliGious beautiful uGly rich or poor for your life he will kicked down doors and break down walls

(time to lauGh in the face of the beast it's our turn to feast at the table we built and wasn't allowed to eat)

No surrender no retreat toGether we can't be beat once we realize that no other race will never ever be able to compete next to us they will be obsolete carbon copies of what's elite from head to feet which is we the melanated people made in the imaGe of G.o.d. this most powerful and holy i say this confidently and boldly when melanated people unite we will concour this land of ours back from beinG stolen from us more quickly than slowly but we must focus on investinG and owninG instead of killinG and hoeinG that's why they created red-lininG and zoninG to block us from seeinG our moments that the almiGhty has atoned us we are from royalty not slavery no lonGer must we pay mind to what they told us history can only repeat itself if we keep on allowinG our enemies to be the teacher of us and our children

(melanated men with open eyes can't Get roped in by white older Guys aka the devil in disGuise)

Men that are wise don't fall for material bribes from white criminal minds that are far from divine cause they are the devils desiGn no heart no spine just Greed and lies and they Got our melanated women takinG off their clothes they have lost themselves no class no pride just ass and thiGhs and they have these melanated men puttinG on dresses instead of suits and ties these are men on the outside but Girls inside who call toys their rides Good women their slides and leave their children to die while they sit on the side as there dauGhters strip and prostitute and there suns Get twenty five to life in some white mans slave institute because they were absent from their lives

(when the mind is free the body can breathe but when the mind is trapped the body will collapse)

When a mind is free it can do thinGs physically and mentally never seen like turn dreams into reality with limitless possibilities like completinG task without retreatinG from it once left to it will be completed properly but minds that are trapped can't think loGically they only have one track thouGhts and that's to think violently common sense missed them obviously cause they are Grown adults behavinG like toddlers be which is a total atrocity to themselves and society in its totality this is beyond a traGedy to children across humanity broken families leaves kids damaGed mentally and emotionally cause they are lackinG the love they were supposed to receive so in love they no lonGer believe because by love they have been deceived so many times especially by family and this happens constantly by trapped mentalities

(mostly everythinG tauGht to us about our melinan is completely neGative and that is totally irrelevant compared to all of our accomplishments)

Before we were slaves we were doctors scientists architects and builders of pyramids and caves healers creators and surfers of waves nothinG was created after us just recreated in their ways since these devils were free from the mountains from which they came they have not for one minute ever behaved they have destroyed so many of us then Gave us the blame when they are the ones whom started the fire and threw us in the flames all because of our melanated frames and our hair that Grows upwards like crowns which Gets its nutrients from the suns rays we never came from slaves we are the descendants kinGs and queens until we had that title stolen away and turned into niGGas and bitches that that don't know how to behave

(no man should make any woman make him feel less because he can't afford to buy her somethinG that she can't and won't even buy herself)

Any man that allows a woman who has not achieved success herself to tell him that she deserves a successful man is not a man he is just a shell of a man destined to fail for any man that puts a woman before himself is destined for jail any man who truly wants wealth will restrain his self from any woman's realm cause most of them will turn your heaven into hell the flesh of these clueless classless women is Gonna Get so many melanated brothers killed by Gunshots or somethinG that will make them very very ill since they love how that raw pussy feels they will end up with the short end of the deal with somethinG that they will never be able to heal

(women are so easy these days all you need is a car and some money and they are willinG to open their leGs to themselves most of them are a plauGe)

$\mathcal{N}$o more do men have to work hard to Get in a woman's draws you don't have to have class morals or principles anymore once you Got some dead presidents they are willinG to open up their doors so many of them are ready to Get on all fours they don't mind beinG whores puttinG more mileaGe on their vaGinas than cars that be on roads all for material thinGs like baGs and clothes and concerts tickets for sold out shows so many women are a total embarrassment truth be told their hearts are cold that's why for a lot of them its so easy for their bodies to be sold cause they no lonGer have a soul and they are younG and old their vaGinas has been throuGh more men than vehicles been throuGh tolls they have lost their Glow easy come easy Go they soon will realize it really does not pay to be a hoe any women that sells or shows off their bodies are extremely slow this they need to know

*(so many melanated men have lost their scruples
Grown with children but still actinG like pupils)*

Men are like boys these days all they do is talk and play dress up like women and pretend to be Gay since when did melanated men beGin beinG this way to find real men in this era is like findinG a needle in hay its like the real men has departed and left the little boys to stay these are men that are still callinG their house cribs and who still play a whole lot of Games men are creators innovators not pussy chasinG lames boys run behind little Girls who run behind fame while real men are busy healinG from childhood trauma and pain but boys wouldn't understand that cause they have no true knowledGe of themselves in their brains of their solar enerGy they are beinG drained little do they know that the more women they have sex with the less time they will have maintain the wealth they have and want to obtain they are ten toes down on the concrete but zero toes down for their family which is insane most definitely

(block parties are now held in cemeteries cause that were most of the youth from the blocks are dead and buried)

The blocks are empty and the frame that holds the soul is also empty hearts so cold it can freeze immediately without feelinG a bit of sympathy endinG a life for them is done so easily violence for them comes so naturally they accumulate more bodies than they do deGrees cause this is the way they were tauGht to be by their no Good oG's they are the new crash test dummies most of them won't even make it to eiGhteen but if they do it will be doinG time in state Greens where the only surround sounds they hearinG is the c.o's irrate screams no eatinG what they want no flat-screens just killers trannies and draG queens now on the block its desolate of children but filled with dope and crack phenes so now the cemetery is where we throw parties for our younG melanated lost kinGs

(if our melanated people want nothinG but smooth sailinG we first must introduce healinG)

We have all been throuGh pain of harsh beGinninGs so many of us are the masters of losinG at winninG the Game for us already started in the ninth inninG born the children of Gods imaGe from start to finish stronG and far from timid the real deal far from Gimmicks so rare and hard to mimic but some how they found our liGht and dimed and put dark within it and it turned us into heartless men and women who now breed ruthless children that do more killinGs than the indians Got done by the pilGrims from royalty to villains for ourselves we no lonGer have feelinGs the devil has possessed many of our melanated people souls and turned them into vermins his new found serpents all for desiGner merchants innocent virGins Get manipulated by frivolous purses that compare to them is totally worthless but these are weak minded women who don't understand what their worth is until they catch somethinG that will leave them earthless cause all diseases start from the inside not the surface so many people are worried about the corona and monkey pox but still Go raw with any and every person yolo riGht until when that illness hits their surface then it's oh no riGht but it's too late then to reverse it now it's funerals and hearses

(there is no rewind in real life whatever you do is sealed tiGht)

Most don't understand until it's all said and done no more turninG up senseless fun no more palm trees and sun from the decisions that was made when we are younG iGnorant and dumb those same decisions will have a lot to do with what we become its always what we do not where we from no matter if it's the suburbs or the slums so many of us are so stuck in our ways until we Get cut by God's blade for joininG the devils masquerade but for so many its too late they done sealed their fate they now have a permanent date with Graves for the moral-less and classless ways they behaved when they had access to all the knowledGe in they world but still chose to be satan's slaves so they will also have to feel satan's pain and this is point blank period simple and plain they didn't choose wisely so they will forever sleep in the mist of satan's flames

(vision less insiGht will only turn our melanated children into the devils prototype)

Could you imaGine seeinG nothinG but carnaGe walkinG out your house and seeinG nothinG but GarbaGe where cominG back home with your precious life surely isn't promised where the hallways and staircases smell shit piss and vomit GrowinG up in a place where they constantly and consistently are subjected to violence all that's tauGht to them is obeyinG and survivinG they know nothinG about livinG cause they are to busy tryinG to prevent themselves from dyinG poverty surrounds them like the belt around orion while there parents are out there shuckinG and jivinG attemptinG to live their second childhood this behavior from Grown adults is totally terrifyinG cause who are the children supposed to be influenced by when their own mothers and fathers out here wildinG

(we are what we eat we are what we speak we are what we hear we are what we see)

Whatever we eat we become so whatever we eat we must make sure it's from the earth from which we are made from whatever the speech is that comes from our tonGues weather to ourselves or others make sure it's positive ones whatever we hear with our God Given ears be sure it words of peace love and care not hate jealousy & fear and whatever we see with the visions we are blessed with allow it to be beautiful and festive instead of violent and corrupted for before the chanGe can been seen on the outside of us it must start with what's inside of us that does not belonG in us such as the neGative thinGs we purposely view the neGative words we spitefully consume and viciously spew the posioned dead flesh of innocent animals that so many of our melanated people call food all these bad thinGs must be eliminated from the thinGs we do

(smokinG mirrors which displays acts of terror of melanated action fiGures that makes the liGht minds of melanated children Go from briGht to dimmer)

1. It's like we ain't Got no more fiGht within us we have embraced becominG spiteful sinners always talkinG about we don't like some niGGas or how much we want to take the life from niGGas the same niGGas who Grew up without fathers fiGures just like them who were also raised by bitter mother's that never even wanted to be bothered with them who didn't raise them to be proper children cause they was busy outside beinG pussy poppinG women hop from man to man they should be called Grasshoppers women and then on top of that they allowed their own dauGhters and sons to witness their classless livinG from when the day starts until it's very ending

(too many seeds planted in bad soil that's why the crops are so spoiled)

When a seed is being planted the soil can't be tampered with or the fruits that seed bares will have rotten fruits on every branch on it no fruits will ever be ripe on it, it will have bugs and mites bites on it pesticides sprayed on it to effect the growth of it no matter how much fruits the seed produces it will always be sour and non conducive with no nutrients included in it and this is exactly what's going on cause grown men are putting their dicks in toxic women and wonder why they are having toxic children once the woman is no good she will most likely pass that on like the plague passed to the indians by the pilgrims kids growing up with absolutely no feelings cause the soil they were planted into was posioned from the beginning after a couple of nuts these weak men are done and finished leaving their offsprings to be thugs and society's menace

(when you are easily manipulated by flesh you will never be able to perform your best this is a messaGe to all melanated men)

Sex is not for leisure or pleasure it is for reproducinG the world with people whom will make it better warriors fellow God's and Go Getters but it seems like so many melanated men rather Go Get her they just think in sex they just think who is next lil do they know that they are cursed and hexed the more women they enGaGe with will be the less they'll be successfully blessed cause most these women are liabilities not assets they are just there to take but not brinG a sinGle dollar in only weak men succumb to these type of women that front like they into them but they are only in to what they can do and Give to them but since pussy controls them they will Give their blood sweat and tears up to them women that had a bunch of dicks up in them

(easy women will eventually end up makinG your life hard)

The easier a woman is to Get the more turmoil you will end up with but some of these men are delusional thinkinG that they are the only men a lot of these women are totally and really into they thouGht that she was just easy for them but she is also easy for him and him too these women Get off with makinG men look like dam fools these women are only their to use and abuse those dudes for their financial on top of that they stay on the menu at every restaurant and venue with fake hair fake bodies and fake faces to they are selfish and unGrateful with terrible diets of process and dead foods but this is what easy women Gets you besides a shallow mind who bases everythinG on her sexual cause she is far from intellectual she has no class nor principals she is senseless to what sensible these women has Gotten more dicks in them than classrooms have number two pencils

(women are loved for bodies while men are loved their money)

Nobody is loved for their brains their character or their kind ways everythinG is physical or material these dam days everyone wants a ride on satan's waves and blatantly disrespect God in his face there is no lonGer no love in this hateful place where so many melanated women are sellinG their bodies while so many melanated men are beinG buried in Graves or catchinG a case what a disGrace after how far we done came we should all be ashamed the way we behave after our ancestors were beat burned sodomized and enslaved and we choose to act like people whom came from caves with all these brutal and savaGe ways some of us can't be saved and will be slayed for choosinG dark niGhts over briGhter days their blue skies will be turned Gray and in the dirt they will permanently lay

(when the flesh is not valued it is sold and shown at hiGh volumes)

So many of these women just like men should put on clown shoes cause they are doinG exactly what clowns do entertaininG their master by actinG like dam fools fake hair like clowns do painted faces like clowns do and walkinG around thinkinG it's oh so dam cool all their thouGhts were Given to them mostly in the white men schools they were educated usinG the white mans tools so now they move like the white man do cause the white man told them to so now they use their flesh in ways God wouldn't want them to from plastic surGery to senseless tattoos these certain melanated people broke every sinGle last one of God's rules just to be abused but since they are Gluttons for the devils punishment when God comes to punish him he will punish them to you can tell the one that don't believe in God by the thinGs that they do like kill each other and take off their clothes for the likes of men they don't know and never knew these are all traits of desperate coons

(breathe throuGh just like a disease do and leave you feelinG weak and feeble like an injection that's lethal)

The amount of evil in people is no lonGer hidden its see throuGh its so twisted that when you tell the truth they don't believe you illeGal is the new leGal and its only Gonna Get even worse this is just a little preview some of us are not God's picture anymore they are a copy of what the devil redrew so now we have a bunch of me too's who choose to not to do what God would want them to do cause they have been well Groomed by the luciferian school to act like puppets and move like fools puttinG their private and personal business on social media like its news some of our melanated people have lost their screws the have become animals in the devils zoo they have become an inGredient in the devils stew they have been posioned by the devils brew to do what the devil tells them to so their death like his will be painfully inevitable since compared to God they think they are more incredible God will turn into dirt for fruits and veGetables cause in the eyes of God their behavior is was and has been unacceptable what they have done to themselves and others is unforGivable cause there bodies have become like houses with a whole lot of rats and roaches in them it is no lonGer liveable

(the Gifts surrounded by curses in neiGhborhoods flooded with churches)

Religion serves a purpose which is to brainwash every and all persons who wishes to participate in the teachinG of mans versus sinGinG and dancinG durinG church services preachers pastors and priest collect money without deservinG it just to buy baGs shoes cars watches and different desiGner purses with it for their wives and different women tax free orGanization reason beinG cause they are manipulatinG people with the scriptures written by white men in powerful positions all to concur people who have melanated piGment and turn them back into havinG slaves cause their minds has been totally condition and Given a western vision of vain-ness and materialism that's why we have so many mentally lost melanated men and melanated women

(understandinG brinGs peace and lack of it makes the cipher incomplete)

Whenever you know the most essential thinG in life which is knowledGe of self and wronG from riGht it will illuminate the dark with liGht but when you lack common sense and simple loGic you will never ever retain a sinGle profit you will only drain your pockets just to just to remain beinG objects to the white mans projects and throuGh his process you will never proGress just reGress and so many of our melanated people refuse to see this slaves they continue to be this it's like they rather be whipped and treated like shit than flee the Grip held on them by the true niGGas which is them europeans demons whom is seekinG to sterilize the melanated woman and steal the melanated semen and eradicate us from ever beinG all for a vision Given that so many of us should have never believed in but this is what happens when a race of people allows oppressors to clothes and feed them they also allow them to deceive

(holes Get duG in cemeteries cause another life Got snuffed out unnecessarily)

Everyone wants to act and be so tuff until they are returned to dust by Guns that bust held by hands that lust and minds that have been corrupt to Get turned on by the siGht of another melanated brothers blood the averaGe child wants to be a bitch and a thuG sellinG ass and sellinG druGs all for the love of what never was but what was purposely made up and not by the creator but by the ones he created and that's why they are so mentally outdated cause love is the answers but so much melanated people have been filled with so much hatred hopeless and faithless GettinG their bodies done and their face lifted all for iG snapshot onlyfans and twitter ratinGs there loyalty is only to deceased men who once enslaved our ancestors without payment so much of our melanated people have become lame men and weak women and they will suffer for everyone of their bad decisions

(the less women you have sex with is the more that you will be blessed with)

So many of our melanated brothers are valueless cause they rate themselves on how many used up pussy they stick there God Given dicks in so much boy behavior in Grown men they think by havinG sex with a slew of women makes them more of men but it makes them less than men cause any woman with a pussy can Get dick from them they are not exclusive men they are men controlled by the flesh of classless women stickinG one of their most precious Gems in these toxic women just to braG and say they slept with them little do they understand that their solar enerGy is GettinG sucked dry out of them by these particular women who are filled with problems and std's up in them moral-less and characterless mindless women will be the demise of so many melanated men for senseless thinking

(look at me im naked takinG off my clothes is the best way to make it these are the word spoken by so many melanated women of this Generation)

*1*t's sickeninG the condition so many melanated women are in its like they have been possessed by a sexual demons GivinG up their bodies for material thinGs that they were tauGht to believe in showinG off their ass and tits for a shoppinG trips to neimans from royalty to heathens from prestiGious women to pussy sellinG minions this is a fact it is not a opinion so many melanated women have been brainwashed by this feminist movement i have yet to see any improvements all i see is a bunch of melanated women naked and screwinG while there sons and dauGhters are dyinG and losinG they busy out there makinG different men use them and this is all of their choosinG to allow men to physically and mentally abuse them then blame the man when it was their choice to open up their leGs to him

(the decision you make today will come back and haunt you tomorrow)

Thread liGhtly or you just miGht be done shiesty well not miGht be but most likely you see most people bark but karma bites be deadly and very few are physically and mentally ready for the consequences of the thinGs they did and said already the tel-lie-vision has manipulated so many weak and feeble minds feedinG them an illusion to Gas them up like Getty so many melanated women want to be like (meaGan) but none like (betty) and so many melanated men want to be like (future) but none like (marley) conscious men and women whom thouGht and moved Godly but so many of our melanated people have joined the devils army for the love of material thinGs such as Gucci fendi louis vuitton chanel and amiri purchasinG over priced Garments but still livinG in poverty and this happens constantly no wonder why melanated people are not where they are supposed to be cause they spend on their wants more than they do on their needs

(the path chosen will determine the karma Given)

When we rise we are Granted with a chance and a choice to keep quiet or display our voice and speak up for what is wronG versus what is riGht but so many of our melanated people think wronG is riGht but since they think in darkness they will be blinded with his liGht for allowinG lucifer to allow them to lose God's siGht they will be hit with pliGht after pliGht after pliGht all the days of their lives they will receive the punishment themselves or it will be Given to their child for their refusel to stop movinG actinG wild Grown men sleepinG with lil Girls that can be their dauGhters and Grown women sleepinG with lil boys when they can be their mothers a bunch of pedophilia GoinG on with a lot of our sisters and brothers all made normal by white men their new fathers

(when a melanated child is tauGht by their oppressors they are automatically beinG tauGht how to act and think lesser)

So many melanated parents are at fault for sendinG their children to learn from a slave cult if they themselves were tauGht to be wokers what do they think will be their children results a educational system is a total insult to the innocent fraGile minds to come it is not their too make them smart it is their to make them dumb it is their to teach them not to embrace their culture it just teaches them how to worship them devil worshippinG pieces of scum the caucus mountain is where their from everythinG they have was stolen from the melanated children of the sun from the land to the invention it was our ancestors it all came from the caucasian people are actually homeless they have no home or culture of their own they just take other people's own and claim that and that's one hundred percent pure facts

(so many melanated men demote themselves to the lesser to try and impress her and so much melanated women deGrade and devalue themselves for a mans wealth)

So many melanated men play themselves on the daily basis just to Get with women that so many men already seen naked their pussies are no lonGer sacred cause it is never vacant always has a tenant in it but their never stayinG and these are the type of women that so many of these men decide to lay with and have bay bays kids with now that is just shameless and so many melanated women will open their leGs just cause of men new whips his street credibility and his community dick then have the nerve to think that they are exclusive when to them same men they are useless except when it's time to physically use them they are completely far from conducive they are only around for a Good screwing

(enemies of ourselves humans are a virus to themselves)

The Greatest virus are humans themself not only do we disrespect our body's we also put our minds throuGh hell all for GeorGe washinGton and benjamin franklin and all the rest of them dead men on them bills when it comes to us we have absolutely no chill it's always kill kill kill so far Gone that now fake is the new real always packinG new steel to let off Gun shots that will never heal humanity is mentally so sick and ill we take and create thinGs to kill ourselves off from posioned liquor to posioned food they Give to us and we just consume it until our doom now ain't that foolish humans themselves are the ones whom do this and for the love of material thinGs and dead flesh so many are eatinG themself to death a animal is Gonna make them take their last breath due to their obvious iGnorance they put before their health but since they don't like to listen simple warninGs God will show them himself cause those who don't hear do feel like

(lack of respect for ourselves will never Gain us the respect of anyone else)

The melanated man and woman is the least respected cause we refuse to respect each other but we respect thinGs we base success on thinGs that actually means absolutely nothinG such as cars and clothinG most of our melanated minds have been frozen with stupidity cause the enemy knows that knowledGe is Golden so if they feed their minds with foolishness they can totally control them and mold them into beinG their minions with the visions they have shown to them and the lies they have told them but when a race of people don't respect themselves nor their own race it is easy to run all over them and one by one take their lives away from them throuGh the food the Graves and the prison system that was made specifically for them to enslave them aGain and mentally physically turn them back into primitive women and primitive men

(money and violence don't mix just like pussy with a bunch mileaGe is no lonGer worth it)

From how the looks of thinGs are GoinG so many melanated brothers and sisters are not mentally GrowinG and it's physically showinG they just killinG and hoeinG melanated women showinG off their bodies and spreadinG their leGs open for material thinGs and paid pleasurable moments while the melanated man is out here drinkinG fuckinG anythinG with a pulse and smokinG as if that is the key to life their minds and ability to think with common sense and simple loGic has been stolen therefore its a whole lot of melanated weak women and melanated sweet men out there like zombies roaminG obeyinG everythinG their white masters told them and behavinG in the foolish way their oppressors showed them they have went from God's creation to satan's children

(capture the mind and the body will follow reason beinG so many minds are shallow and their bodies are hollow)

Once the mental is finessed the body will be next it will be put throuGh stress of thinkinG it ain't blessed from the thinGs shown to the eyes that is transferred to the memory bank where the information is stored cause your eyes are used to record thinGs that it saw so if all it sees is nothinG but war then it will automatically adapt to that no matter the pain that it cause and just like the eyes the ears are also used to record sounds it hears and the frequency levels it's on so when it listen to songs the music must be calm cause the brain reacts to melodies and tones so no wonder why so many of these children are out of control cause the devils music done stole their souls all for the love of money and Gold

(when the devil can't Get close to you he takes away what means the most to you)

How the devil works is throuGh pain and hurt also throuGh desperation and thirst he loves when we shoot and twerk cause it shows our worth which is jail and dirt with dead faces of so called love ones on our shirts actinG like we truly care for the ones whom Get murked but it's too late now cause death cannot be reversed nor repaired cause they done left this earth now that feelinG of emptiness we feel ain't nothinG worse we value thinGs like watches shoes and purse but we forGet to value people until their in a hurse in a coffin leavinG devils church GettinG driven to a cemetery where a bunch of tears will be dispersed but just imaGine we used that ounce of prevention first so much death could have been avoided that can no lonGer be reimbursed cause now their bodies are lucifers dessert

(when the vision is Given by the dead not the livinG death will be the endinG to all the pretendinG)

None of this is real and we should all be offended cause the vision they Gave is not God recommended it is one that has condemned melanated men and turned melanated women into material demons boys beinG raised by Girls in women's bodies who have no clue what their doinG that's why so many of them out there blatantly shootinG violence is their only solution so many lil Girls choosinG onlyfans and prostitution cause they see their own mothers do it but can't only blame them Got to blame the silly so called men that screw them knowinG that they don't have an absolute thinG to offer no children but a mind filled with pollution of reality tv mixed with drill and trap music which is mentally useless mother's are supposed to be the first nurturers and teachers but instead they busy out here beinG GossipinG attention seekers while there sons and dauGhters are beinG introduced to the Grim reaper

(america is in trouble)

America will crumble america will succumb to the wickedness america done did and still do america has to pay for every senseless murder from animals made into stakes and burGers to melanated people put on crosses and burned up america is in trouble for every rape and torture for every kidnap and capture God will make america feel his rapture for the mistreatment of innocent melanated people america will feel the pain of its evil the evil of sex traffickinG america is not united it is a divided establishment that only caters to white men for that God will strike them with more than just liGhtninG God don't like uGly so God most definitely don't like them and their uGly lies will come back to bite them and anyone who stands by them so many of our melanated people will perish with them for sellinG their souls to non melanated dirty old white men who will never respect or like them

(never put bleach on color we've learned that from our mothers)

Bleach and color don't mix cause bleach actually destroys it simple loGic and since we mixed bleach with our colors it totally disrupted and corrupted our melanated sisters and brothers bleach only mixes with white clothes when it mixes with dark clothes it turns it albino it has melanated people lookinG like a sideshow dilutinG our color is their end Goal certain dna's ain't meant to be mixed cause it takes the authenticity away from the melinan that is rich with nutrients that it Gets from the suns rays reptilians and God's do not mesh that's like mixinG a cure with a plaGue then expectinG to be healed of that plauGe but the only way to do that is to totally eradicate that plauGe or separate our melanated selves indefinitely from that plauGe until it eventually disinteGrates away and never aGain Get a chance to live to live another day

(delusional melanated beinGs with minds proGrammed by european)

These are not melanated people we are seeinG they are just white people with melanated skin but ain't nothinG melanated about them cause the white man/woman done brouGht them and turned them into them for instance look at the melanated woman she always quick to wear the hair of some other woman because she does not even want to be herself from plastic surGery which is blatant perjury they want to be everythinG else except what God made them to be which is queen and the melanated man most of them worship white women as if they are the standard the pinnacle when they are far from that they are actually the lowest of the low and that is a complete facts but so many melanated men are under an extreme mind control so they will never believe that we have lost so many melanated people to the vision of white trash

(we are the chosen ones who were cursed but it's time to reverse that and Give them their curse back)

First and foremost we are not black never been that we are melanated Gifts from God don't ever forGet that sin was Given to us we were innocent before we first laid eyes on this earth but since then we been trapped in a vision of lies and riff raff proGrammed to think black which means absence of his liGht also meaninG not a factor in this life in order for the curse to be lifted our people must unite if we ever want to Get this thinG riGht they stole everythinG from us and sold it back to us for that alone we should have been tiGht that's the type of disrespect that deserves a ass whoppinG from the suns liGht to the moons niGht our power lies in our toGetherness our separation is the reason we lose fiGhts our iGnorance is the reason history keeps on repeatinG itself in our lives cause we refuse to open our eyes and see the devil in God's disGuise pretendinG to be him so he can manipulate our minds and take the liGht out of us so we can no lonGer see our shine

(meaninGless banter is equivalent to beinG diaGnosed with a terminal cancer)

A bunch of rappers and dancers actors and GanGster history eluded to advance them because they forGot to become men they have a Grown man's body with little boys trapped inside them father's huh most of these boys that are now men never seen them so they have not a clue on how to be men therefore they have no idea how to treat women that has to be tauGht by the example of a man leadinG but all they have seen is men leavinG and not takinG responsibility of what was reproduced by their semen now they out here talkinG about their demons all cause their father's were niGGas and their mothers were heathens they both left their offsprinGs nothinG to believe in not a thinG else but the streets intriGues them they kill without reasons they either end up in prison or Get left leakinG and eventually end up on a cold mental table no lonGer breathinG cause for all there wronG doinGs God had to Get even

(the pain we endured just to become niGGers and whores)

Look at us they cookinG us lockinG us up and bookinG us like fish they puttinG hooks in us and all we want to do is eat smoke drink and fuck somethinG is absolutely wronG with us after all that they took from us our names our freedom and we have the audacity to be shootinG us instead of salutinG us we stay bootinG in us when we should be soothinG us from all the torture and beatinGs they do to us it's a wonderful life for everyone else but a Gruesome one for us all we do is brinG harm to us like we forGot who we were made in the imaGe of love is Gone from us at least it is for us seems to me we done Gave up on us how could we do this to us it is time that we start choosinG us or we will continue losinG us we make everyone else wealthy except for Guess who everyone of us it is time that we start brinGinG wealth to us and start helpinG us our heaven is here once we stop GivinG hell to us

(we must have forGot we Got God in us cause we continue to be devious)

HealinG is a major factor in our melanated communities from all the hurt that they done brouGht to you and me from rapinG to killinG our lives have been GivinG no meaninG and we are now numb and no lonGer have no feelinGs from Graves to cold prisons these are the two places we often visit because of our blantant refusel to listen to words of wisdom that will put us as a whole in better positions too much selfishness in our melanated men and women we are more kind and Generous to people who constantly try to kill us we are a cursed people who disperse evil on one another on a daily basis we destroy our own community's without thouGht we follow the blueprint the slave masters tauGht we don't even fiGht for each other like our ancestors fouGht the only time we have any remorse is when we Get cauGht we have become mentally physically spiritually and emotionally lost

(before they celebrate you they rather destroy you before they help elevate you they rather deploy you)

Watch people closely and you will truly see who is for you pay close attention to those who iGnore you cause those are the ones whom you have to remove from anywhere near you they fear you they rather Guns air you or the white man jail you a sickness takes over your immune system you with nothinG to heal you they rather lions tiGers and bears tear you knives cut you if it's up to them it's fuck you they would love kidnappers to abduct you they wish absolutely no love for you just sluGs for you or odinG on some kind of druGs for you there only prayers are those of neGative outcomes for you they want nothinG but sufferation and pain for you everyday that they rise they are plottinG on you like bees they want bullets to swarm you like animals they want to farm you they'll even send beautiful women to line you

(so many lost souls will soon find a permanent home at them crossroads)

*T*he penalties that are coming to all those melanated people who chose to be street hoes is something they will never recover from they will most definitely end up in six feet deep holes in their european clothes since they wanted to be Gods foe God will show them that he's beyond cold those who cannot comprehend that will be shown directly since they don't understand how life Goes since material thinGs are there life Goals they will be stripped of everythinG before the niGht Goes even before their eyes close no more liGht shows just dark woes since they dare oppose the almiGhty God code and became selfish no Good humans who lack morals character and class those melanated people will soon be exposed and one hundred percent permanently disposed

(those who don't hear feels)

So many of our melanated people are Gluttons for punishment cause even thouGh they have two ears and one mouth they listen to nothinG until God comes for them now they are willinG to listen but it's too late God is completely done with them it will be no more fun for them just darkness no more sun for them since they forGot to share God will not leave a dam crumb for them since they were selfish with the funds the almiGhty one Gave to them he has a six foot Grave for them since they wanted to be slaves for satan God himself will slay them for certain for them it will soon be curtains since they want to live as serpents God is most definitely Gonna hurt them for allowinG you devil to curse them he will permanently dirt them and exit them from earths realm

(first we use fiGht for a cause now we fiGht for applause)

We use to be leaders now we have become foolishness doers we stay disrespectinG ourselves and our own for washed up wrinkled old white men approval it's no honor amonGsts our melanated people to each other we are evil and deceitful we hate one another but love us some white people even thouGh they consider us 3/4 of human and far from their equal yet we still wear their Garments that is brandishinG their last names to them we are one biG Game to bad so many of us do see their aim it is us that must refrain from continuously puttinG ourselves to shame with nothinG to Gain but prison time and a early Grave so many soulless women and heartless men done sold themselves for the price of fame it is not the God in them they worship it is the satan in them that they claim but since they represent lucifer hell they will die in his flames

(the fallinG of a Great nation cause instead of beinG men their busy on iG or on their play stations)

Fatherly duties they done vacated havinG sex with females they just want to play with but don't plan to stay with these are not men these are lame pricks who one day will Get sick for thinkinG with their dicks from one of these salmonella contaminated chicks all just to say they hit they will deserve whatever illness they Get these type of men are rookies not vets their is no evolution in them they are still mentally children in the bodies of Grown men raised by bitter mother's and father's that disowned them so instead of beinG different than their fathers were they became them these low down pieces of absolutely nothinG of substance should never be called men cause men are leaders these dudes are followers of all trends ain't a bit of leadership in them all they do is smoke drink and have sex with random women not knowinG if they Got the monster or some other std's in them

(so much melanated heathens and attention seekinG demons)

So many are not livinG their just breathinG so lost in the thinGs they are proGrammed to believe in until they are lyinG there dyinG and bleedinG for the lifestyle they were leadinG those who wants to be seen are the ones that Get left leakinG for beinG the devils puppets and minions popularity and fame is what's Gonna kill them cause before they accomplish their own Goals they let all know their vision but this is what happens when one wants attention they put themselves in terrible position over and over aGain because of their iGnorance and refusal to listen God will seek them personally and have them swim with the fishes or buried in ditches for beinG disrespectful niGGas and bitches instead of what they truly are which are kinGs and queens princesses and princes

(the trouble so many women are in for participatinG in these seven deadly sins pride, Greed, lust, envy, Gluttony, wrath, and sloth)

1. no pride whatsoever it's like whatever

2. all Greed puttinG their wants before their needs

3. the lust for material thinGs thinkinG that love has to do with a size of a rinG

4. the envy they have toward their own Gender so many of our melanated women are the biGGest pretenders

5. the amount of Gluttony in them they are willinG to Go out with mostly any man willinG to feed them steadily indulGinG in unhealthy over eatinG

6. the wrath of God will humble these women in ways they cannot even imaGine for the thinGs they have done to their God Given bodies all for sexual attention

7. the sloth in these particular women will leave them sinGle and lonely for beinG mentally shallow fake and phony

(when the fake is embraced the real is erased)

What's GoinG on riGht in front of our face is fake beinG loved and real GettinG hated nothinG is real no more not there body not there hair and not there face we have totally destroyed this place with fake personalities moral-less behavior what a disGrace there is not disease worse than humanity itself ain't not virus worse than the virus of humanity themselves physically and mentally puttinG themselves throuGh hell for white men on paper bills now tell me that ain't siGns of people that are mentally ill callinG themselves niGGas and barbies worshippers of the devil cause ain't nothinG about them Godly the are now part of the devils small army but all those fake thinGs and people will soon see how brutal God be for everythinG they have done and did God sees and anGry is an understatement to what God be so many of our melanated women and men will be brouGht to their knees for participatinG jealousy Greed sloth and envy

(oh what a terrible web we weave by believinG in make-believe)

So many of our melanated people have allowed themselves to be cauGht up in a web of lies from a bunch of old white Guys with Gray blue and Green eyes these white men have no melanin inside and without melanin there is no way they will survive cause they are not divine they are not of Gods desiGn of any kind and they never were at no point in time and never will be we tauGht them how to be clean then they over powered us and tauGht us how to be more like lucifer and less like elohim they tauGht how to be mean to each other and praise them like they are really kinGs and queens when they stole that title from the likes of kinG tut and queen nefertiti then they robbed us of the land that we used to feed them truth be told never did we need them now to all my melanated people it is time to leave them no lonGer should any of us want to be them work for them nor believe them cause they are the true niGGas and heathens

(these are not men these are spineless moral-less cowards)

Social media Got a lot of these so called men movinG real funny similar to how women move for money these are not men these are male version of their mommies stay with an attitude move and act like dummies but they will soon be brouGht to reality from the punishment that is cominG for these boys in mens bodies there sunny days will turn cloudy for beinG slaves to pussy and rowdy all for the love of dead white men money these men have lost themselves in the illusion they all wrapped up in it like some mummies they have become like white boys miGht as well call them tommy always quick to catch a body always outside instead of beinG inside with their family that's why death finds them easily cause they are always in places that they don't need to be

(i Guess a.i.d.s don't exist no more cause everybody is out here beinG promiscuous whores)

Aids must have went away so many melanated women playinG russian roulette with that Gift from God that's in between their leGs until they Get cauGht with that deadly plaGue that will never Go away that is here to permanently stay since they want to experiment with their bodies this way as well as so many of our melanated men have also Gone astray and Give their bodies up just to Get a nut from a female with a pretty face and a biG butt but a small and shallow mind that does not have one bit of intelliGence in it of any kind but are willinG to catch a std cause on the outside she looks fine but on the inside you can tell her vaGina been in many rides it has no class no morals and no pride her club done been shot up too many times her vaGina is no lonGer divine

(so many of our melanated people have lost themselves in the white mans vision therefore they will forever be trapped in the white mans prison)

Look how the white man winninG look how the white man Got us doinG the white mans sinninG look how the white man GrinninG as he's fuckinG our beautiful melanated women and imprisoninG our melanated men and children look how the white man has as livinG Got our melanated men soft as twinkie fillinGs cause when it comes to the white man the melanated man bows down to them but when it comes to another melanated brother they be drillinG and spinninG these clowns are not of God they are the devils minions this is facts not opinion cause God would not destroy himself that is the devils mission but all those who went and Go aGainst God there deaths will be violently vicious

(i write for the pain in us and for all the days it rained on us)

Things has never been simple and plain for us Guns constantly aimed at us nothing but flames for us and neGative names for us this is most definitely not what God wants for us it's like we ashamed of us always chanGinG us for the love of the lust in us cause we certainly don't Got love for us cause look how we be treatinG us at this point nobody is defeatinG us more than we are defeatinG us the amount of hate we have for us could not be measured by no scale cause it now out weiGhs the hate that the white man once has for us now that hate is displayed by us no more do they no lonGer have to rape rob kill disrespect dishonor and disGrace cause that to is also done by us until we are turned into ashes and made into dust no more must we do this to us

(the devil will be put to silence for all his senseless violence)

For each and every soul out there wilding killing robbing and selling their bodies they will understand soon enough exactly who God be the devil may have a Gang but just know God has a army of militant men and women that move think and react Godly not men and women who hang out on streets or in building lobbies you see God sees all this is not a maybe or probably so all those that continue to fly in his face will have their wings clipped for violating God's Grace and most precious Gift which is the life he Gives and the body that we are in he allows us to still live after everything so many of us has done did im talking about pure foolishness like for one all this senseless shooting being done by these kids and for two these Grown adults that is not doing absolutely nothing about it and for three countless women who put their bodies up for sale and men who pay for them God will soon end all their fairytales and bring their fiction back to real

(show it all off melanated woman leave nothinG for surprise melanated woman)

So many melanated women have lost their way now they have become the devils prey but it is them that wanted it this way so it is them that will have to pay for strayinG away from Godly ways and pickinG up devilish ones they better repent now or deal with God's wrath because of how they treat their Godly bodies like trash they are no lonGer like them powerful queens of the past they Give their bodies up fast for baGs shoes and cash then have the nerve to braG like they accomplished somethinG Great when little do they know they sealed their own faith all for the leftovers on someones else's plate all to be in some rich white mans faces just to end up beinG the white mans waste what a absolute disGrace to our melanated race

(we have become pussy all soft and Gushy)

Oh we touGh riGht we the savaGe rouGh type catchinG bodies in broad dayliGht to kill each other we be so hype but to kill our true enemies we take fliGht how is that alriGht how is that at all riGht its like we lost all siGht no love for each other just all pliGht so much hate for one another but for the oppressors all bark no bite but when we see our own brothers we be ready to take their own lives life is stay sour it never Gets ripe from warriors to now male version of their mothers with a more vicious Gripe constantly bowinG down to everythinG that's white we kill each other everyday and our community does nothinG but if a cop kills one of us we ready to march and write from the wee hours of the day to wee hours of the niGht all talk no fiGht

(the mental is empty cause the vision does not exist)

If nothinG is shown or nothinG is seen then that would only mean there's nothinG to be dreamed just broken promises and humanity's absence of elohim bunch of followers of the devil reGime those same followers will also be faced with the same consequences for joininG esau's team and becominG killer prostitutes thuG bitches and druG phene this is the new in scene this is the new norm for our kids see profound behavior from Grown adults that is supposed to Guide them to be better human beinGs but instead they are GuidinG to be vain materialistic lovers of europeans the same people that killed our ancestors and considers us melanated people to be cattle feed they have raped us hunG us beat us separated us and left nothinG for us but hate Greed and lust in us we must Get the white mans vision out of us or it will definitely be the permanent death of us

(weak men are attracted to weak women therefore breedinG weak children)

Only a weak man would want a weak woman who puts a price on the most precious thinG she has in life and only a weak woman would allow a weak man to run up in her all for a seafood dinner and if the man is weak and the woman is weak what the hell do we expect from the children but but to weak just like their parents be too many men want easy women cause they have no challenGe in them and weak men just like weak women are the reasons we have so many violent children cause weak men and weak women have absolutely nothinG to teach but how to turn up and Get hiGh and drunk on the weekdays and the weekends weak men and weak women lead by the most deGradinG and terrible example all they do is talk shit post pics when in reality their lives are in shambles their brains are completely fried and scramble and there offsprinGs has to pay for their costly Gamble

(when no pleasure can eliminate the pain inside)

As long as the pain remains inside happiness will never be able to be seen outside until one finds the root from where the pain resides and destroy it then from one the pain will never divide one who holds on to the pain will continuously allow that same pain to rain on their own parade pain is their daily plaGue a mental illness that won't seem to Go away cause so many choose to hold on to it everyday allowinG it to Get in their way of their reward of pleasure God wants to send their way but first they must let Go of the pain let Go of the hurt so they can receive all the Gains and blessinGs for the pain they went throuGh as a adolescent but first they have to eradicate that pain from their essence cause in that pain is a lesson that once one fiGure it out they will be able to experience their Gifts and presents

(hiGher earninGs beGins with hiGher learninG)

The more you follow the less you Get the more you know the less you sweat a wise mind makes money in no time because it knows itself but an unwise mind has to beG sell and steal because it has the thouGhts of someone else other than oneself therefore it will never obtain true wealth knowledGe is powerful no wonder why so many are powerless cause they lack knowledGe and all the benefits it brinGs wealth beGin within ones inner self without the belief the sacrifice consistency and discipline one will never truly enjoy life wonderful experiences and the whole bliss of it cause they have no real knowledGe nor clue of it but the one who does not know but is willinG to learn will infinitely be able to earn

(niGhtmares on them streets worst than fredddy Gave you niGhtmares on elm street)

Ain't nothinG on them streets sweet you either Gonna end up a stripper prostitute a killer a druG dealer or a no Good niGGa but to the streets you will most definitely be a loser you body will be use in dirt like they do manure then somebody will be replaced were you was the streets will either turn you into ashes or into dust one thinG that the streets don't have is no love it just lusts for the blood of bad bitches niGGas barbies and thuGs the streets is ten times more ruthless than any human ever was but all those whom think the streets is were its at will be reminded violently they should have never thouGht like that cause so many of our people went on them streets and didn't make it back

(s.t.d. sexually transmitted demons)

When you are havinG sex with a person you are also havinG sex with every one that the person done had sex with to take a risk like that is more than thirsty and desperate it is also classless and it just shows how valueless and worthless that person truly is demons has possessed their very skin now the devil dwells within so many wonder why they can't win cause they are filled with demonic-ness in them they have tarnished their whole existence cause they can not resist the temptation of havinG sex with the devils vaGrants and for that they will be plaGued with the sexually transmitted demons that they chose to sleep with those are weak women and weak men that let's sex control them and for that God will most definitely scold them

(the creation of a delusional function that has most of our people's minds filled with nothinG but dumb shit)

From tik tok videos to naked ones and these are Grown women with dauGhters and sons who are supposed to be leadinG by Good examples but instead they are leadinG by bad ones very very sad ones this is definitely not what God wants this is what the white man wants cause as lonG as the melanated man and woman are separated the white man won if we don't start to stick toGether our demise will be the lone outcome Ghetto is not a area it is a mentality that we must escape from we are Gods creation therefore we were meant to create but instead when end up as food for worms in dirt Graves all cause we continue to be slaves and misbehave our iGnorant ways will have us extinct one day cause we choose to have the devil use us as his prey cause if you look outside it is us and our children whom are GettinG slayed we have been the victims of the white mans savaGes ways no more must we be victims it is our time to make them pay by any means necessary like malcolm says

(she has a whole lot of drinks in her and a little bit of think in her)

That liquor makes her wine her evil spirits that's why it is called wine & spirits cause once it enters her system her mood intertwines with the devils elixir now she inherits satan's devilish mixture of becominG promiscuous and sellinG her videos and pictures even becominG a stripper once she's drunk off that liquor she'll let basically anyone lick her and even stick her without protection now nine months later a baby delivered out of lust not love now it is that child that has to fiGure it out cause she don't even know who she let sleep with her was a life chanGinG experience she's willinG to risk it all just for a buzz of a concoction that is meant for her to let her Guard down and Give herself up now it will be her that will be stuck because she drank lucifer posion and forGot who she was

(what did they all die for, for us just to die more)

Children are born and not beinG cared for so most of them will never reach their true potential nor their rare form cause all they are tauGht is to be violent and bare arms they weren't Given love just told how to survive within this world storms no joy just bitter mother's and father's that's not there for them so many of our Great leaders and younG children has died in complete vain only a couple of tears sheds for them then the madness continues with no end family turninG aGainst family and friends killinG friends this is not the order of God this is one hundred percent the order of satan the envy the jealousy the Greed the hatinG all of it is lucifers creations to prevent us from our divine destination of peace tranquility and a hiGher mind elevation

(we came up foolish listeninG to GanGster and druG dealinG music)

We made neGativity our influences so positivity were no lonGer use to it we rather hear about a shootinG or somebody dyinG to us that has become exclusiveness even though it's not conducive and makes all our melanated people look uneducated and stupid cause we are better than the thinGs we are doinG and if we don't wake up and smell the coffee yet another Generation will be ruined for lack of evolvinG all by our choosinG wastinG precious time on social media sites like it's real life pretendinG to be happy but in real life that's not at all what it feels like cause true happiness could never come no man made up sites cause it comes from inner not outter and when we realize that then we will beGin to start truly livinG our lives with peace in our hearts and riGhteousness in our mind then we will once aGain become divine

(any woman that needs to be taken cared of should be steered clear of)

Any woman that doesn't have for herself shouldn't be expecting from a man nor no one else especially if she's not putting that same energy into herself but thinks because of her looks and body she's deserves some mans wealth or some mans help when the circumstances she is in she brought it on herself then wants to blame everyone else but herself how dare does she even have the audacity to point a finger at another person when three of those fingers is pointing at herself but her refusal to take accountability will only allow her to keep on repeating herself until she becomes insane and it starts affecting her health you can always spot a woman that does not treat herself well she always on some site offering her body for sale when she does that she automatically fails all because she considered fake to be the new real

(from extraordinary fiGures to hoes pimps bad bitches GanGster savaGes and averaGe niGGas)

We never use to have these thinGs in us once we became these thinGs we became sinners and as lonG as it remains in us we will remain killers of ourselves and our kids kids kids future all for the approval of the devil lucifer cause God would not most definitely approve of this from us we have become the forGetters of love we are now the embracers of lust time to chanGe the neGative views that they have about us and return to the royalty we once was no lonGer must we think below we must now think above cause the melanated man and woman been the outlets and the pluGs therefore it is time to take back the heaven they stole from us

(soc-lie-media is no different than tel-lie-vision)

These are two places where one can pretend to be someone else other than oneself a place where one can pretend that they are rich when in reality they are poor as a dried up well with not a pot to piss in or a home with a widow to throw it out as well bunch of fake happy people that has nothinG to do with their lives but take pictures and films proGrammed by a vision that has been Given to them by their true enemies to brainwashed and block their creative cells which will allow them not to think for themselves our men women and children have been misGuided to embarrass themselves for little to nothinG of the white mans wealth so just like tel-lie-vision soc-lie-media is also bad for ones health

(enemies of ourselves therefore we don't have to be the enemies of no one else)

No more do they need to kill us cause we do it to ourselves no more do they need to rape us cause we do it to ourselves no more do they need to beat us cause we do it to ourselves no more do they need to pimp our women cause we do it for ourselves no more do they need to mistreat our children cause we do it for ourselves no more do they need to abandon us cause we do it to ourselves no more do they need to put us throuGh hell cause we put ourselves throuGh hell ourselves no lonGer do they have to fail us cause we are failinG by ourselves no lonGer do they have to exploit our black women our black women cause our black women exploit their selves themselves no more do they need not to support cause we do it ourselves no more to they need to hate on us cause we do for them to ourselves the weiGht we put on ourselves can break any scale no one on this earth has never felt the pain we feel and when will we realize that we need each other then we can beGin to heal

(number one draft picks to Get their ass kicked)

From then to now we are the last pick especially when it comes to this planet resources we are less fortunate we Get little to no portions for us it's slow motion Grand openinG Grand closinG once it's black own our own people will make sure it don't stay open you can't even let your own people know you own it cause they do everythinG in their power not to support it or if they do always want a discount even thouGh they can more than afford it but then will Go to the european desiGner stores and spend a whole fortune just to be walkinG billboards for the slave masters Garments they do not need to advertise it themselves cause black people Gives them all the free promotion for one hundred percent of all their food and clothinG

(i cry tears for my peers who no lonGer exist here life is not fair just beinG black is a absolute niGhtmare)

This is madness everyday another wiG split another younG boy dead before he even Gets a chance to dam live nothinG but sadness younG Girls sellinG their bodies like it's worthless actinG like it's only for sex they serve purpose and no one is doinG absolutely nothinG about this hurtinG cause no child was born Guilty they were made into that person by not seeinG anythinG but poverty stricken neiGhborhoods filled with thousands on top of thousands of serpents so they must become venomous themselves due to their circumstances otherwise they will have very slim chances of advancinG in the chaos they were lusted into without beinG Given no answers by the two people that are supposed to protect them the most and show them the ropes but by them two people they have been the most abandoned

(we are from the land not the man we are plants trees water and melinan) for whom that does not know

*H*ere let me tell it then we are earths (dauGhters) and suns (sons) of elohim therefore we are divine like him with the ability to shine like him turn water to wine like him create and desiGn like him we are aliGned with him once we combine with him and take accountability for all our sins then we will beGin to individually and collectively win like him cause the devil will be Gone from within hate will no lonGer live in the system now love can enter in and do its healinG and seal the crack in our hearts from all the losses of senseless killinGs of our men women and children similar to how the indians Got done by the pilGrims just to steal them and their land from them and snatch away from them God's freedom

(we movinG blind and losinG time)

Everybody just wants to shine even if it means exposinG themselves on or offline women naked all over social media cause they think beinG naked means that their sexy and fine and to add to that a bunch of Grown men with lost minds who think with their dicks at all the times but women allow these type of men to enter them then play victim to their crime of them lyinG to them to Get in between their thiGhs when they already knew he was not a man of the Good kind but more of the hood kind they could careless about the beauty in a woman's eyes when they already Got their minds on their prize which is what she shows most so she will be seek for that most by desiGn and by the time most of us realize we are playinG ourselves it's too late and we're out of time

(the last lauGh will be had by God for all those whom are doinG the devils job)

God will have the last lauGh i hope those people who went aGainst God are prepared to Get lauGhed at for beinG lab rats Guinea piGs actinG like low class trash showinG money cars tits and ass the white man is havinG a blast makinG each one of us a thinG of the past they depict us as thuGs niGGas bitches and everythinG that is bad and then we continue to treat each other like dirt which is totally sad after all our ancestors been throuGh and sacrificed for us how dare we repay them like that their deaths must no lonGer be in vain they suffered too much pain for us to be actinG and movinG this insane for baGs shoes rinGs and chains if we don't chanGe our ways one by one we will see our early Graves for the ways we choose to misbehave and continue to be their slaves

(either we keep crashinG or start leadinG in a elite fashion)

We need action or the white man will continue thrashinG bashinG and smashinG us for their satisfaction we are a bunch of jokes to them that's why they keep lauGhinG cause they know whatever they do to us our women or children nothinG will happen cause we black men are to busy trappinG our Guns is too busy clappinG killinG our own where's the loGic our women are too busy twerkinG and our kids are physically and mentally hurtinG and none of us is workinG towards killinG these serpents then and only then will we Get rid of these curses that's landinG us black men in jail and hurses and have our black women sellinG themselves for shoes and purses for us this is not God's purpose in God's mind we are worth in the white mans mind we are worthless it's time to prove the white man wronG and reverse this or continue beinG left earthless

(what are we doinG here look how are we movinG here)

So many of these adults be actinG weird they are behavinG without a care while their children don't dream they have niGhtmares cause love from their own parents is not their too busy on social media showinG off their bodies and fake hair while Grown ass men on the same social media showinG their money and new Gear they should stop callinG it a new year when the same thinGs are happeninG from the old year miGht as well call it a no year but by the way we are killinG each other soon none of us will be here from the bullets that penetrates our skin to all the process foods alcohol that we put within we are the killers of ourselves it is not only white men we have to do better by us if we expect to Get done better by them then the disrespectful way they treat us will most definitely end

(the damaGe we've done to our dauGhters and sons and continue to do cause we refuse to improve)

Look what we have become from royalty to claimers of slums Gun shots is our new anthem we went from beinG smart to beinG completely dam dumb our women have become whores and our men have become dam bums and they have the nerve to hook up and have sex and add children to them now their children out here killinG cause they weren't willinG to tell them about the God born in them cause they have no knowledGe themselves they rather shoot rob kill and sell themselves you can't tell me this ain't hell this place is were the devil dwell cause God would not allow us to do this to ourselves only satan would stand around and watch us continue to fail and lauGh and dead souls as our bodies start to turn pale

(our vision must be impaired cause apparently we ain't seeinG clear)

We must be blind if we don't see what they doinG here either we are foolish or just don't even care how did our ancestors with less have no fear but us with all the resources we have we act like there is nothinG there we have become scared back then they had Guns and our ancestors had all but spears and they still won their just for us to lose here we pimp our women kill our brothers and abandon our children here picture beinG left in the wilderness without the proper Gear then GettinG approached by a Grizzly bear either they learn how to concur fear or Get ripped and teared and their blood smeared everywhere and they are all alone no parents there now in their hearts imaGine the resentment there

(we are all in for a rude awakeninG for forsaken him we all about to see the true powers of elohim)

So many of us is takinG God for a joke i hope they are ready for all the smoke since some of us decided Give up on faith or hope souls so dirty it can't even be washed with soap they have done sunk their boats all to be niGGas and hoes all for fame jewelry and desiGner clothes they also buy and sell their bodies somethinG that God would have never chose but the rude awakeninG that is cominG for all of those who opposed his Goals they will soon see the power that he beholds death will soon be cominG to anyone that thinks the devils way is the way to Go they will be left lonely stiff and cold weather they be younG or they be old no one has ever escaped the karma of the most hiGh for beinG the most low

(a pretty face and a fat ass cannot raise a child neither can Good pussy and a beautiful smile)

So many boys in mens bodies will choose a woman with a banGinG body and Good looks over a woman that is intelliGent well put toGether and in to her books who can teach their children to be somethinG other than strippers niGGas prostitutes and crooks now who has to suffer from the choice that they took the children that are now off the hook beinG raised by Girls in women's bodies who don't know how to clean or cook i blame particular type of so called men for thinkinG with their eyes and dicks rather than their brains and their common sense for if those little Girls in women's bodies that they choose to put their privates in is barley capable of providinG for themselves what do they think they can do for someone else these type of women literally put their own children throuGh hell and are a major reason why they end up in Graves and in cells from beinG bred by waterless wells where the fatherless dwell as humans so many of us failed is like we lost the ability to feel

(bad bitches birds and barbies Go for men with bread real women Go for men with character Goals that are spiritual and Godly)

There is two types of women the Godly and unGodly you can tell the difference between the two cause one is covered up and the other are always showinG off their body a real woman you have to earn them other women could careless as lonG as you have money in your wallet they are willing to let you touch them and even penetrate them for dead men whom no lonGer consume a body basically whorinG of their most precious commodity what a atrocity it is time to once aGain Give real women notoriety and kick these Gold diGGinG no Good women out of our society

(from the most miGhty to the most weak from the most rare to the most obsolete)

We use to be the miGhtiest ones the rarest ones the most intelliGent and fearless ones now we have become the weakest and spineless ones the careless and the hard of hearinG ones the non carinG ones the no love for ourselves but love for money and material ones the hateful ones the unGrateful ones from the faithful to the unfaithful ones the fearful ones the the ready to kill each other but scared of the white mans Guns from royalty to the ones that now claim the slums we rather be called thuG niGGas savaGes bad bitches barbies than the kinGs and queens of kinGdoms how could we ever allow this to happen after all our ancestors did to represent us they died for absolutely nothinG cause look how we treat us no lonGer is it the white man it is us that defeats us cause we refuse to love us

(infatuated by material thinGs)

The infatuation for material thinGs has our people wastinG their money and time with thinGs that are irrelevant to their divine they think they need jewelry to shine when they already have the jewelry inside these desires has our people behind cause they feel that they only look Good in european desiGns but that is a thouGht of a insane person that has lost their mind they are not intune with reality of no kind their minds has been proGrammed so their eyes are totally blind to our enemies lies for these material thinGs so many of our people died cause they fell for thee illusion of these wicked white Guys they never been for the betterment of us only our demise when will we realize they want us black people to all die every black man every black woman and every black child you see before they concur they must divide the powerful and stronGest people this or any other earth will ever find

(from riches to raGs we were robbed of everythinG we once had)

We were never slaves that's what we were made in order to take our Godly powers away we were tauGht how to misbehave we were tauGht how to be bitches and niGGas and Godless fiGures by white men who are here to kill us and put us in Graves they are not to be trusted in any sort of way cause they will befriend in order to infiltrate and then do everythinG in their power to prevent us from beinG Great they are the ones who tauGht us hate and don't want us to procreate cause if we do that will mean thee extinction of their entire race they cannot stand our face their plan is to totally eliminate us from this place we must never allow that in no which way

(adult kids)

Adult kids look how these adults live look what these adults did supposed to be adults but act like dam kids resulting in the chaos were currently living in cause we refuse to change from the ignorant ways within adults are leading by such a terrible example on social media making a mockery of themselves as children do acting like belligerent fools thinking that shit is cool when there's sons are getting chopped down they are are on instagram moving like clowns while there daughters are becoming hot thots exposing themselves for boys in mens bodies cause they believe that their bodies is all they got the mental condition of adults these days has their own children seeing early graves all for attention while there kids die in vain this is a crying shame these adults don't care about their children they care about fame

(followers of the devil will be crushed like rocks do to pebbles)

A lot of people will soon Get a rude awakeninG for forsaken him and instead embracinG him the devil the creator of sin i lauGh at those people who side with him cause they to will die with him since they want to ride with him God will show those demons whom follow satan how quickly he will eliminate them all those fake women and fake men women whom take their bodies and mutilate them and men who don't value their bodies either so they Give it away like it's nothinG these are acts of the devils functions these acts are not of God nor should they be considered anythinG close to it but these individuals God is directly watchinG them and will soon put a permanent stop to them for not understandinG the power of him the almiGhty elohim it will be absolutely no pity for them weather they be man or woman they will soon meet their end

(material slaves and attention junkies)

Slaves to material and junkies for attention no different than the druG addict needinG a fix from his/her druG of preference an addiction is an addiction no matter what form it comes in and a slave is a slave if they decide to side with this materialistic misGuided dumb shit that needs to be eradicated and done with we are the children of God not the devils minions this is a fact not an opinion and until we stop beinG attention addicts and material slaves we will keep on beinG disrespected in every which way from beinG injected with plaGues to taken our God Given abilities away but it is up to us to stop them from treatinG us this way by lovinG ourselves and one another every and each day

(so many of our people put their wants before their needs and wonder why they always need)

So many of our people find pleasure in putting their wants before their needs like for instance a man does not need if it's just he and a woman don't need a birkin or chanel bag if she still mentally and physically in poverty only children put their wants before their needs either them or adults with children mentalities who are still mentally sixteen their priorities are backwards their behavior is awkward they rather be niggas and bitches instead of black Geniuses and black nerds any adult who put their wants before their needs should automatically get curved cause they are mentally delusional and thinking completely absurd in every sense of them words

(zero days versus thirty to thirty one days)

We are the richest broke people to ever exist we rather look rich than actually be it soon as we Get some money riGht away it is leavinG out of our communities and beinG sent into the communities of our enemies these white demons who from day one has been tryinG to stop us from breathinG the playinG field is far from even cause we are choosinG to be niGGas and heathens we must put aside our differences to once aGain be maGnificent as black people we need each other in order to lift this curse that we have been Given by the God of sin which is satan within we have been proGrammed to think less of us and more of them no more must we allow the devil to be responsible for how we live its is time that we stick toGether and finally put this slave treatment to an end no more beinG haters of one another and lovers of them

(look at us then look at them we are each other's enemies they are each other's friends do you see the difference between us and them)

We are not for each other we pocket watch and hate one another as if we are not brothers we have been broken and separated by our oppressors to look at ourselves as lesser instead of leaders if we can chanGe the way we view ourselves they could never beat us cause little do we know they actually need us we don't need them cause no us means their end and any more of us to be born will completely eliminate them for existinG this is why they create diseases and sicknesses to vanish us from livinG they Give posioned food to our children and abortions to our women if we don't chanGe our ways they will continue winninG and we will continue to be sent to prisons and Graves for beinG physical mental and material slaves

(the pain inflicted left us lost and conflicted)

The pain inflicted left us lost and conflicted that we no longer value ourselves as kinG more like dick swinGinG barbarians we use to be valuable and prestiGious men until the day we let the devil in and eliminated God from within our holy realm which is our inner self all for made-up wealth we kill each other and even ourself we are the only ones puttinG each other throuGh hell in Graves and in jails cause we choose to be iGnorant therefore we choose to continue to fail cause we think real is fake and fake is real but due to the pain inflicted so many of our brains are twisted thinkinG fiction is realistic

(time will reveal the truth in a person)

Time will reveal the truth in a person watch and listen cause in time a person will reveal to you your position in their lives you can see the lack of respect for you in their eyes they are only around you for a free ride to Get their and Get a ticket to Get inside but once in they forGet that you were the one that Got them in from outside they constantly try to out shine they also constantly cross thin lines they are not on brouGht only borrowed time one hundred percent users who shouldn't be considered to be family or friends at no time cause those people are that of the devils desiGn soulless physically and spiritually with poisonous minds

(the acts of men now will determine if they are fortunate or if they will suffer tomorrow)

The acts of men now will determine is they are fortunate or if they will suffer tomorrow God will have no pity nor sorrow for piercinG a man chest with his deadly arrow for not followinG him the almiGhty sparrow any man who disobey's God's direct orders should be held accountable tortured and slauGhtered for not beinG a Good friend a Good brother a Good man a Good sun or a Good father a man is determined by how he treats others when he is in position to help others if a man does not followinG the rule of God which is to help his fellow brother he deserves to be under white sheet covers

(the future depends on lessons that are learned today)

The future depends on lessons that are learned today the future ain't looking to good for us or our children cause we are busy being niggas and bitches while our children are prostituting and killing no longer are we parents to our children to busy on social media glorifying materials things and disrespecting ourselves and our very own black women many boys in mens bodies will say they do to themselves but that don't mean that you got to perform the act with them if a woman is not being a woman never choose not to be a man with them just dismiss them cause once you stick your dick in them you become a part of them and just like they are lost you will be lost with them pussy have cost so many brothers lives to end

(the devil is God here)

The devil is God here cause God wouldn't have his own children living in mans fear how can God be here when there is not a soul on this God forsaken earth that actually has a dam care God is love and i don't see a bit of love here only hate and niGhtmares no compassion just darkness and death stares soulless men that only cater to flesh here polluted minds from the devils illusion spread all throuGh the dense air everyday for over one hundred years the devil is in total control here unless we rid our minds of him so we can once aGain will be able to see clear and realize our purpose for beinG here

(pussy and Greed will brinG many men crumblinG to their knees)

Pussy and Greed will brinG many men crumblinG to their knees too many men put pussy before even their ownselves not knowinG that that's doinG a disservice to their own self all for a piece of pussy that more than likely smells and that many other men ran throuGh it like coins in a wishinG well between a woman leGs is were the devil dwells that's why after you fuck it, it puts you throuGh hell all for a piece of used up beat up bruised up tail it is the Greed of man why he constantly fails never sharinG information or intel for that thinGs will not end well his body will be used by the dirt for its stem cells

NiGGas die everyday as they should cause a niGGa is a niGGa and a niGGa is no Good all he does is think hood eat hood drink hood rob hood kill hood he is trap in the chaos of his own thouGhts and in his iGnorance he will be put into a coffin that's all wood and buried in the same dirt that they threw on loyal dudes a niGGa don't deserve no respect why should he when he disrespect his ownself by allowinG neGativity within his own self he creates his own hell any man who sides with a niGGa or have niGGa ways they to will also fail for the blantant violation of Gods holy Grail they will be sent to a early Grave for beinG a niGGa slave to the white mans wicked ways

(most of the time your family ain't really your family your just related to them)

These days it is your own family that will see you starve they could careless if you here or Gone but understand this that blood don't make you family it just makes you related loyalty and love makes you family and friends are more family cause family be hatinG who shut you down more than family anytime you came up with a idea or creation friends ride with you family never wants you to reach to your destination they don't support you but quick to use you for their own interests without hesitation these days who needs enemies when it's your own family that will do you dirty with not one ounce of procrastination so be careful who you call family cause everybody don't view you how you view them and that's a fact that one day you will have to come face to face with that your own family is the ones that be hatinG

No mercy for the selfish may they feel the wrath of God for their sins aGainst their own family and friends may they Get done to them as they have done to so many others in secret may they be buried in the same hole they have duG for others for beinG heartless demons may they be reminded that they cannot escape the karma of their doinGs and as they have brouGht destruction on to others their own lives will soon be ruined for not evolvinG with evolution and continue the devil mind pollution as if it is the solution death will soon be their conclusion for believinG in the devils illusions

(pussy controls a lot of these clowns)

Pussy controls a lot of these clowns they be ready to Give it all up just to Get down with some chick that has been passed around all throuGhout town they are willinG to lose their own families for some used up washed up pre-owned old pussy the devil in the form of a woman that can manipulate a weak minded man so quickly cause she knows that he thinks with his dick and one day it will leave him so sickly from a std that can't be cured such as h.i.v. these dudes be playinG russian roulette with their dicks constantly and consistently and not thinkinG about the diseases they may contract that will live with them permanently all for some hoes who have no self respect and low self esteem heathens and peasants not nubians and queens these dudes rather stick their dicks in dirty pussies instead of ones that are clean no different than fuckinG a crack head addicted to methamphetamines

Sacrifice and discipline breeds power he who wants power and success will sacrifice for it he who doesn't will allow pussy to have him distracted from it cause they are to busy thinking with their dicks more focused on pussy than money even though pussy comes with it pussy is a want it is not a need the only thing that's a need is a mans health and a mans money pussy chasing is for unintelligent dummies who is performing under a low frequency both mentally and physically psychologically and spiritually pussy controls these men pussy is their majesty pussy will also be their tragedy so many men have lost their lives chasing used up washed up pussy instead of their own destiny

(how many women that done had you determines your value)

How many women that done had you determines your value so many men no longer have value cause they themselves have been ran through no different than hoes been ran through so that would make them hoes to something of value is rare and not easily obtained something of lesser value is easily given away you are not a man until you can resist what is in between a woman's legs the more women that you have sex with doesn't make you a man it makes you a plague a little boy in a mans body that's chasing aids constantly risking his life for some pussy that's basically old and gray cause it has been used up by so many different individuals ain't no way that it's good no more no way

(shameless brainless and aimless)

Shameless brainless and aimless so many whom call themselves men are really not that cause men don't put their dicks in women that work in strip clubs or that are prostitutes on tracks any man that values himself would never do that risk his own life for whore women who lack the ability to comprehend that what they are doinG is wack and this is one percent facts no real man wants to share pussy only little boys want to do that real men want quality women not women that a bunch of dicks done swam in any man who does such a thinG will lose at winninG for puttinG their dicks in these demonic delusional mentally twisted women and expect them to be proper mother's to their precious and innocent children men must stop stickinG their dicks in these unworthy women who fuck and suck dick for a livinG

(watch closely cause a person will reveal themselves eventually)

Watch closely cause a person will reveal themselves eventually in times of victory and triumph you will not find out who your true friends and family are you do not know who will truly side with you until you Go throuGh war or if there is money or women involved only then you can tell if for you they are riGht or wronG cause most people are there only for the use of you if you have no use to them in a blink of an eye they will be Gone these days you can't trust no one especially when it comes to hoes and funds your own family and homies will Get you done so watch closely cause it's your own friends and family that will Get you stunG by somethinG you will never be able to return from

(so many of us has failed as men)

So many of us has failed as men how can we call ourselves a title that we do not represent correctly one men don't lie especially for pussy men don't Gossip like women nor arGue with them like charlie brown and snoopy men take accountability not play victim when they are faced with consequences of their doinGs men evolve boys remain childish and foolish men lead by example cause they know its always room for improvement but little boys be on social media showinG their money and Garments they are scarred boys who have yet to become men who really never had nothinG so now that they Got somethinGs they way to show everythinG that is not the way of a God or kinG that is the way of a niGGa a peasant men don't continue cycles only boys do thats psycho men break Generational curses to build leGacy and Generational wealth like God wants us to do so time to manup devise a plan up no more sittinG down time to stand up no more beinG buried in Graves no more GettinG our hands cuffed enouGh is e-dam-nouGh of us beinG touGh to us that only makes it rouGh for us it is about time that we have love for us

(no one has ever won aGainst karma you reap what you sow)

No one has won aGainst karma you reap what you sow so many Go with the flow instead of creatinG and becominG the flow men want to be niGGas flashinG their material Garments and takinG pictures and videos of all their doe women want to be hoe showinG off their bodies always takinG off their clothes but God's karma will come to both of those for breakinG code of the true words that was told but still chose to take the devils road but since these individuals seem not to care God will show them his cold since they want to be bold and mess with his mold no man nor woman can disrespect God and expect not to Get scolded but since they want to follow society's and social media's trends they will have to face the consequences of sellinG their souls to a man called satan with absolutely no soul God is Gonna punish them niGGas and hoes and its a Good thinG that you are not affiliated with none of those foes

(smart dicks don't fuck dumb pussies)

Smart dicks don't fuck dumb pussies that is only done by young rookies whose main objective is to Get pussy similar to how little boys loves cookies no man can consider himself a hiGh value man if he is entertaininG low value women constantly with not a bit of intelliGence in them waste women most certainly danGerous never safe women definitely mental case women literally men must value their physical spiritually cause it is a God Given entity not to be Given away so easily for it holds the seeds of humanity and puttinG it into the wronG pussies has destroyed so many black families cause every pussy is not supposed to be fucked especially if it's not attached to a woman with class morals character and inteGrity no man must risk aids just to Get laid that type of mentality been played smart men don't move in such ways only little boys who are sex slaves stick their dicks in these dumb pussy heathens who have nothinG to offer them but stressful and dark days due to their dark ways

(peace of mind brinGs peace to minds)

Peace of mind brinGs peace to minds a crime starts in the mind for thinGs the eyes have seen that is now permanently stuck in their mind all by desiGn but that can all be chanGed once you Give them positive quality time to realiGn their mind and brinG them back to their divine shine sinners were never born they were made by a vicious plaGue embedded in their dna that makes them act this way but once peace is Given to them the beast will no further live within them and they will Grow from boys to men once they find the peace within them they will no lonGer be victims of the judicial system modern day slavery younG black boys in white owned private prisons where they are Given life sentences with no second chance of livinG products of an environment that they didn't ask to live in filled with prostitutes druG dealers and senseless killinGs all cause their parents weren't willinG to Give a better life to their children

(the madness within the minds of blackmen)

The madness within the minds of black men it's darkness in them from all the violence they have experienced so many losses of friends so much death they have seen boys whom have lost their souls before they became men when they were mere teens life wasn't fair for them mother's out there living their lives father's are absent nobody but the streets was ever there for them there cries for help no one wasn't hearing them now they are deaf to love from all the hate that was displayed to them heart Gone no longer can you play with them cause they are frozen from things that happened to them when they were children that now cause them not to have love nor feelings for themselves nor no woman

(more venomous than any snake is family members and friends that continuously hate)

More venomous than any snake is family members and friends that continuously hate you can tell a fake friend or family member riGht away they are users that will use you up then throw you away for money pussy and fame these individuals are one hundred percent total lames and deserves nothinG but flames cause they are some snakes that needs their heads cut off so they can no lonGer live another day cause they are in the way absolutely pure poisonous snakes who will look directly in your face and line you up to be taken off of this place erased and never aGain be able to be remade you Got to watch who you call your family and friends these days cause they dam sure don't see you that way

(the devils playGround where hate jealousy envy and Greed stay round)

The devils playGround where hate jealousy envy and Greed stay round God was never in control over this planet the devil and the people whom worship him are and have been for thousands and thousands of years now and here's how by turninG our women into to bad bitches and our men into circus clowns who click hop just to be down notice everyone is on demon time or some kind of Godless savaGe time and all this wickedness is apart of the devils mind this is not of Gods desiGn men hatinG on men friends jealousy of friends family no support from them just a whole lot of envy in them related by blood but that's where it ends cause once you follow the devils ways you ain't nothinG but pretend for this is the devils layer his sanctuary his house his realm and he is here to destroy the souls of men and turn them into him pure chaos and mayhem this place is not of God this is satan's playpen

(secretly indictinG themselves then wonder why they end up in cells)

Secretly indictinG themselves then wonder why they end up in cells a lot of dudes be tellinG on themselves by showinG everythinG their doinG for the dea and feds every watch every car every female they brinG into their beds every post on social media GlorifyinG materials thinGs is a set up to fail cause whatever a man is doinG the whole world doesn't need to know the details that's just GivinG them intel to sabotaGe their wholesale before they can sell it for retail thereby cuttinG their inventory short and liGhteninG the load on their scale cause they wanted to let everyone know what they are doinG instead of keepinG it to there selves men that are GettinG indicted robbed and murdered are actually brinGinG that attention to themselves by showinG their heaven while others are GoinG throuGh hell cause the more they show the more that's their to tell and them charGes comes with no bail

(biG steppers no joker business like heath ledGer)

BiG steppers no joker business like heath ledGer black leGends like marcus Garvey the God rakim elijah muhammad malcolm x and the honorable minister farrakhan elite intellectual wise complete men not shallow and weak men deep and unique men never sweet men mind capacity of prophets scholars and brave men above never beneath men, men of a different caliber so you cannot mentally enslave them with foolish european Garments with the names of slave masters on them cause they are leaders not followinG men with more feminine than masculine in them they understand their God Given position spans beyond the thouGhts of man and they would never partake in any white mans shenaniGans that is the definition of a true black man those other dudes are white actors in black faces claiminG to be a black man but that is furthest from a fact man cause those black men have become puppets for them white men just so they could like them

(the breedinG of serial killers)

The breedinG of serial killers head tappers a habitual spinners killinG has become natural so much that they have become numb to the problems that's all within them with no answers to solve them so it is only GettinG worse and no one seems to want to help evolve them from boys to stronG men of that privileGe society and their own parents has robbed them therefore revertinG them back to cavemen slave men no lonGer brave well behaved men cause of the circumstances that their own parents Gave them their was no one there to save them they just had sex and made them then basically played them by turninG their backs on them there father's abandoned them and there mother's resents them because of the hatred they have towards their fathers cause the relationship didn't make it

(Get your banana split like Guns do to heads in a bonanza flick)

Get your banana split like Guns do to heads in a bonanza flick shootouts everyday another man Gets hit bullets enter clips that then enters Guns that Goes on hips ready to rip throuGh the flesh of its next tarGet a bunch of younG lost heartless damaGe men who are in so much pain they want their lives to end because it makes no sense to them to live in this hellish realm where there is absolutely no help for them from family or friends they feel that if they were dead it would end there punishment their lack of nourishment they are thirsty with no water to replenish them all this evil is done to them simply because they are black boys that will most likely never make it to be black men cause on a daily basis senseless murders subtract them it is only violence that attracts them and it is the fault of both parents this happened and continues to happen

(never forGet the blood and the sweat)

Never forGet the blood and the sweat and the ones that left you for dead never forGet the ill thinGs that was said behind your back by so called family and friends never forGet those lonely niGhts when no one was there to help you fiGht never forGet the ones who use their darkness to dim your liGht never forGet the ones that didn't treat you riGht never forGet the ones who made you cry never forGet the ones who never even tried never forGet the ones who had a chance to chanGe your life but chose to turn a blind eye never forGet the ones that used you to only benefit them i want you to always remember them because when it was up to them they considered you to be nothinG never forGet what they did and how they treated you when they obtained material thinGs money never chanGed them it just revealed who they truly is but God will continue to bless you for everythinG neGative they ever did God will return their karma to them if not them their kids and you will have a front row seat to watch all of it

(words are powerful spells when used correctly it will determine weather you pass or fail)

Words are powerful spells when used correctly it will determine weather you pass or fail pay attention to the words you tell yourself and to someone else for words are a reflection of oneself when one continues to use a neGative word to describe oneself one will become that word that one spoke of himself if one considers himself to be a niGGer he will continue to move iGnorant if one continues to call himself a trapper he will always be trapped by his own words if a man calls himself a kinG a God then that man will be that verb a man can manifest his success with these two stronG words which is (i am) almiGhty all resilient and unstoppable in every definition of those words we are the Gods of this earth from the day that we were birthed how did we ever Get in last place when we were once in first i will tell you how "words"

(what is demanded cannot be denied)

What is demanded cannot be denied by any man woman or child for determined men move with a whole different style distinGuished intelliGent Gentlemen with a wild side that is totally under control at all time no small minds that still thinks beinG a GanGster is fine when beinG a GanGster Gets you life either in a Grave or penitentiary for movinG wronG when they could have moved riGht for that God will soon shut off their liGhts their days will no lonGer be briGht they will no lonGer have siGht cause when God Gave them the ability to see they turned a blind eye on their friends and family their will be a punishment cominG to those people beyond what their simple minds can believe selfish human beinGs will suffer the wrath of God for the fucked up people they turned out to be

(value a woman as you would want one to value your dauGhter)

Value a woman as you would want one to value your dauGhter as fathers we must move by a different standard a different order for if we do not the karma will fall upon our dauGhters for what we have done to other mens dauGhters when we knew better but still chose to move heartless just cause a woman is easy does not mean that we have to take parts in it playinG russian with our dicks for undeservinG uneducated and unworthy women who don't have a thinG GoinG on for them but GivinG their pussies up to mentally weak minded men that does not want a woman that challenGes them no wonder why it's so fucked up for these children cause to many men are messinG with easy women who have not a God dam thinG to teach them but how to be heathens like them and these are the women we must stop breedinG and even beatinG cause they are literally demons that wants to use us for our semen

(take away the money most of these dudes wouldn't be shit take away the cars none of these dudes would probably have chicks take away scamminG and druG dealinG most of these dudes wouldn't have chips)

Take away the money most of these dudes wouldn't be shit take away the cars none of these dudes would have any chicks take away scamminG and druG dealinG most of these dudes wouldn't have chips most of these dudes are not beinG loved they are beinG used by women for material thinGs they could careless if your a kinG or a peasant as lonG as you Get them a present they will Give up their essence to whosoever buy them Gifts that's more expensive if these men never had money these women would never want them but these days dudes rather be used like stunt men by Ghetto women who have not a dam thinG GoinG on for them but havinG sex with who Got the biGGest baG for them and these dudes Give them the attention when they should one percent iGnor them cause most of them are prostitutes and only Good for whorinG

(just because we have dicks doesn't mean we have to fuck everythinG that has a pussy attached to it that's some lame ass shit)

Just because we have dicks doesn't mean we have to fuck everythinG that has a pussy attached to it that's some lame ass shit like aids still don't exist and do we think that any of these women who have it is Gonna tell us that shit so many of us be buyinG the hiv cause these women are sellinG the hiv but this only happens to men who don't value their dicks and Give it to hoes and dirty chicks and expect not to eventually catch a std from them and their dirtyness for a man to stick his dick in some unworthy chicks he is definitely not the man he say he is cause a man would not disrespect himself and have sex with a woman valued less than him

(only boys Give themselves up to easy women)

Only boys Give themselves up to easy women cause they ain't Got no challenGe in them no morals in them they think they Got a dick just to fuck a bunch of women but they have a dick so they can reproduce with them but these dudes is busy stickinG their dicks in unworthy women with not one bit of class in them then with these same women these dudes bare children and expect these uneducated women to be able to teach them now the children have to suffer because of one lust filled weekend when the pussy is easy and he still fucks it, it just shows how easy he be just like you are what you eat you also are what you beat so if any man sleeps with weak female then that also makes him weak cause he is mentally functioninG under a very low frequency and will never Get to the pinnacle God wants him to reach cause he is addicted to easy pussy

(this ain't no cartoons it's real Guns knives and harpoons that pierces the hearts of all Goons)

This ain't no cartoons it's real Guns knives and harpoons that pierces the heart of all Goons the way we are killing each other we'll be Gone soon after everything we been through this is what we do act like buffoons consuming their vision and consuming their tunes we have allowed our oppressors to have all riGhts on what we eat what we say or what we do like they are more adults than me and you modern day slavery in plain view brains Get discombobulated with their fake news to make you hate you cause once the black mind is manipulated the white man he can now recreate you into something and someone God didn't make you thereby leaving God with no other decision but to forsake you for making the devil break you and take you off of the course with all the real blessings God had for you

(from the ball sack to be carried away by the pallbearer life of a black man is pure terror)

From the ball sack to be carried away by the pallbearer life of a black man is pure terror imaGine always havinG to watch your back cause it's constantly and continuously always under attack that is the reality of beinG black even our own people treat each other like dirt and crap in actuality and even in rap either we killinG each other in the music or on the block in the trap all because stand up men chose to sit down and allow that now we are in full combat at war with ourselves and our own black brother's and the k.k.k loves that cause no more do they have to be the ones that Gives us our dirt naps we do that everyday with each and everyone of those Gun claps where we take our own black brother's off this earth never to come back now that's dumb wack and that's all facts

(niGGas and heathens savaGes and straiGht demons)

NiGGas and heathens savaGes and straiGht demons you are what you believe in so if you call yourself these four thinGs you will start to be them any thouGhts in your mind that you are any of these words you need to free them if not they will either land you in prison or stop your breathinG those names Given by racist europeans are not names that we are supposed to address ourselves or each other with cause we are not any of those thinGs niGGas where you mean God's and kinGs heathens where you mean emperor and prince savaGes never you mean Gentlemen with wits demons we could never be cause we were made in the imaGe of the almiGhty and we have the God Gene runninG all throuGh our body this is not a maybe or probably we are almiGhty God beinGs so what we manifest within ourselves is what we will turn ourselves into beinG so let's now manifest words of royalty and positivity so we can start healinG and improvinG we are men and as men we need to stop what we doinG and watch how we movinG cause we are beinG watched by fraGile minded children

(no blueprint no map just put in a trap and left with no Guidance nor directions on how to Get back)

No blueprints no maps just put in a trap with no Guidance or directions on how to Get back to who we once were what we once represented which is not this sick and demented thouGht of men with minds of kids how is boys supposed to Grow up if their father's never did sad to say many so called men are at fault for this small minds in biG frames is the reason for all of it followinG the same cycle instead of breakinG it cause if so many of us Grew up without father's and we knew how we felt how dare we allow our children to also Go throuGh it that makes no sense the thouGhts of so many mens minds are absolutely stupid repeatinG the same madness that have our race of people ruined

(he who seeks happiness in his wealth is he that truly does not know himself)

He who seeks happiness in his wealth is he that does not truly know himself for happiness cannot be found in wealth but it can be found in health and knowledge of self not a things else for happiness has nothing to do with anything outside of oneself happiness starts with what's inside of oneself once you turn off everything outside of oneself that you view happiness will take over oneself makeover oneself but so many men think they need a bunch of expensive material things to show and prove what they do how much money they have when they couldn't even begin to know wealth not realizing making money don't make a man out of you how you move when you have nothing do cause any man with money could pay his way through weather or weather not he is cool cause if only money brings one's happiness that means without it one wouldn't know what to do

(what is done cannot be undone)

What is done cannot be undone i hope violaters remember this when they are violatinG the almiGhty one by not followinG his only beGotten sun all for the facade created and Given to them by a race of people that is biblical spiritual and mentally lesser than them but yet they take lessons from them and expect Good results to come out from them how can that be possible when these same men that they listen to is the enemy of them they are despisers of black men from food to Gun to diseases is just some of the many ways they try to subtract them but the funny thinG about this Generation of black men is that they let them just to Gain acceptance from them those are absolutely weak black men

(so many of these dude are better off havinG pussies cause they already move like they have one)

So many of these dudes are better off havinG pussies cause they already move like they have one these dudes Gossip more than women from day to eveninG bunch of chatty patties mouths on yappie yappie always knowinG others people's information happy talk more than a bunch of women at the beauty salon who are divorced sinGle or simply don't Got nobody cause real men don't chat cause they are busy creatinG leGacy and makinG currency they could careless about what another man drives wears or does with his time those are women ways tendencies of men who are secretly Gay cause real men don't think move nor act in such ways

(rich lookinG poor minded)

Rich lookinG poor minded i never seen this much amount of so called men in my life who rather look wealthy than be it everyday wearinG Garments made by europeans and these men are descendants of africans but worship white men as if they want to be them these are not black men they are white men in black skin who have no soul within they will spend thousands of dollars on their oppressors last name but want a discount from a other black men but salute to you my brother for not lackinG common sense like them for supportinG other black men and for beinG a honorable stand up black man

(their is consequences to every action so make sure the reaction is worth the consequences of the action)

Their is consequences to every action so make sure the reaction is worth the consequence of the action many men will suffer the consequences of all the evil they have done to other they will be smothered in their own dirt the same dirt they Gave to another will eventually bury them to cause you cannot do on to others and not expect it to be done on to you no sin is left unpunished none not even one the consequences will be equal to or more than the bad thinGs they chose to have done to the children that came from the almiGhty one which they weren't supposed to do to the children of God and the brothers of the sun for that karma will find them and completely swallow them up for not GivinG a fuck

(mind over matter cause the mind creates the matter)

Mind over matter cause the mind creates the matter like the flour and the water creates the batter like the jealousy and envy creates the chatter like eatinG dead animals made into process foods makes you fatter the mind is such a terrible thinG to waste but so many waste by GettinG up and just beinG basic when they were created to be amazinG but they allow matter to Get in the way of the Gift God Gave by allowinG material matter to mentally enslaved and turned them into caGed men and Grave men all for the love of dead white men who hates them and that every sinGle day tries to eliminate them from existences

(black didn't start with slavery it started with royalty)

Black didn't start with slavery it started with royalty we were never servants of man only of God faithfully but the white man convinced so many of our people that he is their God that they rise up everyday just to do the white mans jobs and worship him Gratefully even thouGh he blatantly wants to stop the air they breathe permanently they rather be the white mans slaves than be the Godly men that they were born to be they have become followers of man and not of G.o.d they forGot that God made the men they follow they are quick to follow man which God created instead of followinG God who created the white man which they follow but they are to cauGht up in white mans illusion to ever understand that this was the devils plan to mentally then physically break the black man so he can concour our kinGdom while they rape our black women and kill our black children like the indians Got done by the pilGrims

(creations were made to create)

Creations were made to create the word create is in creation we can look at it, it's riGht in our face future builders that's here to pave the way with love and understandinG so these kids can have better days difference makers risk takers no lonGer mental slaves. leadinG by a positive example so our children know how to behave no more endinG up in Graves because of the wronG information that was Gave reason beinG so many of the younG youth are lost within this maze of dust and haze done by men demon made men who worship the devil and the evil reality which he displays and continues to replay over and over but it is up to us to chanGe it from beinG this way it first starts with inner chanGe to rearranGe the way we were trained which is not to use our brains therefore remaininG the same it is all a part of our oppressors Game

(when it comes to each other we want all the smoke)

When it comes to each other we want all the smoke but when it comes to the white man it's yes sir no that's why the white man take us for one biG joke who love to wear his clothes cause even thouGh they were the one who put us our position that left us messed up and broke we look riGht pass them and with us we want all the smoke they are afraid of us sleepinG Giants becominG woke so they turn us aGainst each other so can purposely sink our boat and allow it to no lonGer float cause we are too busy GettinG at each other throat all for the love of those dead notes we have forGotten that the boat we have row toGether in order to reach Goal and receive our Gold and take back our souls from our foes

(if the word love was used more often they will stop endinG up in Graves in coffins)

If the word love was used more often they will stop endinG up in Graves in coffins love was excluded out of so many of their lives they were tauGht not how to love but how to survive they never learned nothinG about the birds and the bees just how to avoid GettinG killed on these streets picture beinG tauGht this how are they supposed to live comfortably when they have to move heartless cause they basically was tauGht this so many of them Grew up loveless huGless that's why they care less and move careless and fearless cause when they spoke about our pain nobody wanted to hear them they just wanted to discipline and scare them now they have become animals no one wants to come near them when all they had to do in the first place is tell them they love them it would have avoided all of this chaos these killinGs by anGels turned demons if they actually had someone who told them and showed them they love them they will choose better options they are filled with so much hate and darkness it is only love that can stop this without that their bodies will not stop dropping

(the best is yet to come we are Gods chosen ones)

The best is yet to come we are gods chosen one we are so valuable they kill us just to drink our blood they created guns cause with their hands they could never defeat none of us they know what's up with us made from water sun and stardust we are literally wearing god on us we are shapeless formless we cannot die our father just keeps on reborninG us we have warriors in us but we have been manipulated by lust our hope and dreams has been crushed by the enemies of all us they are prayinG for the fall of us due to the lack of love we have for us we must of forGot that we are the children of the all miGhty one so on that note the best is yet to come and anyone who went aGainst the black man the same aGainst them will be done

Made in the USA
Middletown, DE
28 October 2022